God in the Pub

A Vision for Street Work

Reverend Gerard Vrooland

God in the Pub

A Vision for Street Work

'Blessed is that servant, whom his lord when he cometh shall find so doing.'

Matthew 24:46

The lesson of my deceased parents

Note from the publisher:

In this book the American rules for spelling and quotation marks are followed. In the United States, periods and commas go inside quotation marks regardless of logic.

Titel: *God in the Pub*
Subtitle: *A Vision for Street Work*
Original Dutch title: *De kroeg als Gods akker*
Original Dutch subtitle: *Straatwerk is verbinden*
Author: Reverend Gerard Vrooland[1]
Publisher: Maatkamp Publishing, Zelhem, the Netherlands
© 2015 Maatkamp Publishing (MP)
Translation: Stephen Teeuwen (www.stephenteeuwen.nl/en)
Editor: Hannie Tijman (www.tijmanvertalingen.nl)
Cover: A bar in New Haven, CT, USA, March 3, 2008.
Cover design: Ruben Hadders, Harderwijk, the Netherlands
ISBN: 978 94 91706 25 7

Websites in Dutch:

Publisher: http://www.uitgeverijmaatkamp.nl
Author: http://www.pand33.nl

Twitter account publisher: @uitgmaatkamp

---

[1] The surname of the author, Vrooland, is pronounced as 'lowland.'

Contents

	Preface The Lord is my Shepherd	7
	Introduction Shocking answers	9

The background of the work in Sliedrecht (Chapters 1-3)

1.	What does God do with us and where does He do it? The run-up to Building 33 and COTS	13
2.	What is Building 33? A place where young people can feel at home	17
3	What is COTS? Searching for the unorganized church	27

A vision of evangelism centered on connecting (Chapters 4-12)

4.	What do you mean, 'Stop the fever and learn to connect?' A different perspective on evangelism	33
5.	Why a street pastor and not an evangelist? A brief study of the New Testament evangelist	39
6.	How do you get connected with people? By seeing what God is doing in the other person's life and tapping into that	47
7.	Can a pastor go freely into the world? Yes, because all good things come from God	55
8.	How do you keep yourself free and bold? A brief study of Cain, who lost his freedom	63
9.	How do you communicate love? Your physical presence is the first thing people notice about you	77
10.	What is real love? Let everything about you be a channel of God's love	83
11.	Talking with people as a street pastor? Your conversations will be determined by what you have to give	95

12.	What can we learn from the book of Acts? A brief study on the Book of Acts	109

**Possibilities for connecting
(Chapters 13-17)**

13.	What practical steps can you take towards caregiving? Demonstrate real love by overcoming your fears	117
14.	How do connections come about? Examples of love and creativity	127
15.	How do you find the workers you need? By dividing the work effectively	143
16.	How does someone who was not a worker before become one? A glimpse into the change processes of Alie, Henk and Merel	155
17.	Is it alright to call the COTS groups a 'church?' If we can see the Lord of the harvest at work there, it's justified	175

**The current and future connections of COTS
(Chapters 18-19)**

18.	What is our prayer for the future? Longings, prayers and frailty	187
19.	The COTS fellowship A series of callings	193

Appendix 1. The Good Samaritan — 205

Appendix 2. Thirteen conversation pointers — 217

Preface

The Lord is my Shepherd

The phrase 'The Lord is my Shepherd' is familiar to many people all over the world. It is often cited by believers as a kind of statement of faith, as a way of expressing confidence in the Shepherd's guidance. It's like saying you are His sheep and you want to place yourself in His care. Which is great! But a creed is not just another way to wag your tongue - it is meant to bring our entire lives into obedient action. It has to be lived. He is my Shepherd; I'm not the Shepherd. I don't determine myself where I go. *He* does. *I* am a sheep.

There are a lot of devoted Christians battling away for their Lord. These fighters have not yet fully understood the creed we began with. Their approach has caused a lot of strife in the church. It also appears in how they evangelize. So forced! And often so damaging! You can almost see these believers sweating away inwardly to provide everyone they come across with a perfect and exhaustive summary of the good work of their Lord. They fire off round after round of words to try and persuade others to believe in God. Sometimes they refer to their own zeal as 'just witnessing,' but they try so hard they would outdo the noisiest of market traders. They take up the Lord's cause as if He can't fend for Himself. It makes no sense at all: I've never seen sheep defend their shepherd. If a shepherd is attacked and fails to protect himself, something is badly wrong! The sheep will run for their lives and the herd will be driven apart. They will certainly not stand up on their hind legs like boxers and start using their forelegs to try and beat the attacker. Sheep like that don't exist, and God's children should not try to do that kind of thing either.

A vital lesson I have learned in my work is that the Shepherd Himself is perfectly capable of calling His sheep and adding them to the flock. If I start interfering, failure is bound to follow. All I have to do is to be sensitive to His promptings and to follow up on His instructions. That is the attitude I have to practice from day to day. Only then will the Shepherd be able to do His work.

It came as a huge surprise to me to find that the Shepherd had many lost sheep in bars. God had a field there and I was invited to work in it. The Shepherd was busy there! Speaking of the Shepherd and his sheep, there's an old proverb that says a lot about how sheep learn from each other. It goes like this: 'If one sheep leaps over the ditch, all the rest will follow.'

Normally, a shepherd will herd his flock in the direction he wants them to go. As soon as the first sheep heads out in the right direction, the shepherd will make sure the others follow. In other words, good behavior is for sharing. That's what this book is about. I'd like to share what God has done in my life and in our lives, along with all the forgiveness and mercy that come with it. My prayer is that He will use this book. If He does, all I can do is honor Him. I hope the fact I've written this story in the first person singular will not be too much of a hindrance.

Our ministry in Building 33 and COTS (I'll explain the names later) has involved a lot of people so far. I'd like to thank all those engaged in prayer, odd jobs and volunteer work as well as those who helped us produce this book. Miranda Renkema offered constructive criticism and helped me get through the early stages. Bets and Joke Bot corrected the text and encouraged me to keep looking for a publisher. Publisher Eddy Maatkamp's hands-on, enthusiastic approach gave me the confidence that everything would work out. Above all, I am grateful to our Savior for making all of this possible.

For privacy reasons, most of the individuals referred to in this book do not appear under their real names.

All Scripture quotations, unless otherwise indicated, are taken from the KJV.

Introduction

Shocking answers[2]

Proposition 1:

Violence is on the rise around the world, and Christians are a part of it.

All of the young people agreed.

Proposition 2:

The more Christians there are, the better things will go in our country.

All of the young people disagreed.

Proposition 3:

Jesus said Christians are supposed to love their neighbors as themselves, but hardly anyone shows that kind of love. Christians are just as selfish as everyone else.

Almost all of the young people agreed.

Proposition 7:

Christians have been taught that obedience is a virtue, but because they carry on being disobedient themselves, there is a lot of hypocrisy among Christians. They pretend to be morally upright, but in the meantime they cheat as much as everyone else does.

Almost all of the young people agreed.

---

[2] Propositions 4 to 6 have been omitted (less important).

The young people I'm talking about are a group of ten teenagers aged 14 to 17. On September 22, 2010, they were sitting at the bar in Building 33 (the name of our youth center). Most of them were more or less familiar with the church because of their upbringing. They had a lingering sense of God's existence. So they were willing to come over once every two weeks to discuss topics related to the Christian faith. One evening I presented seven propositions. You just read four of them at the beginning of this chapter - along with the kids' response. Their views on the family of God were quite negative. As I listened to them, I felt a deep sense of shame.

I asked myself how on earth Christians could have such a bad image. I had expected a degree of sympathy from these particular teenagers. Sure, I knew a few of them were anti-Christian. But I was convinced some of the other members of the group would offer more positive answers. I couldn't have been more wrong! My hopes for a debate between protagonists and antagonists were ruined. Instead, what I faced was a demonstration of unanimous negativity. It was painful, to say the least. I tried to say a few nice things about Christians, but it only put me in a difficult position. And I wanted to share the gospel on the street!

The question as to how we should share the gospel in our day and age has occupied me for a long time. Teenagers like the ones I described above know churches have evangelistic outreaches. But they're not interested at all. That evening I heard some confronting comments. I tried to find comfort in extenuating circumstances. They're young, I told myself. They don't have a proper grasp yet of what Christians do. They're unaware that the diminishing levels of trust among people in our Dutch society are commensurate with the drop in the number of people professing faith in God. They don't know there is a proven relation between faith and happiness, trusting God and trusting people - and that if the one drops, the other does, too. But none of these considerations made me feel any better. I knew there was something wrong with how the church manifests itself on the street. But what?

This book is my modest attempt at exploring some new avenues. Whoever is familiar with the richly varied history of the church will recognize that these avenues are really not new at all. I believe they are paths we must rediscover with fresh creativity. Thankfully, a lot of Christians nowadays are involved in this kind of pioneering. To me, this means the Spirit is leading us to a fresh creativity, with increasing urgency. But creativity is not the only thing. We have to learn to reconsider our place in the world and our perceptions of people. In this book, I'd like to try and share how we can look at people differently, so that God will be able to help us really connect with them. These are the things I'd like to encourage you to think about. I'm not out to criticize conventional methods still being used by churches and evangelists; if it sounds if I am at times, it's just because I want to make things clear. Please forgive me if you think I'm being insensitive! I'd also like to ask you to forgive me for sometimes giving you the impression that in the search for new angles I'm the guy who knows it all. I'm not! I'm searching. And in everything we do, we are deeply dependent on what God gives. In and of myself, I'm a lost sinner and it is only by God's grace that I can seek His will at all. I'm thankful that the ultimate judge of my attempts is a loving God.

The background of the work in Sliedrecht[3]
(Chapters 1-3)

This book emerged in the context of our creative search here in Sliedrecht. We - that is, a group of Christians and myself - are trying to reach out to people who have never had any kind of connection with the church, or who have turned their backs on it. In the first three chapters, I'd like to describe the setting in which we undertook our search. I will then use that backdrop to describe the search itself.

1. What does God do with us and where does He do it?

The run-up to Building 33 and COTS

Sliedrecht is the town in which our search is set. It covers an area of 13 square kilometers and is populated by over 24,000 people. Sliedrecht's claim to fame is its performance in the dredging business. It is situated in the Dutch Bible Belt, a stretch of the Netherlands known for its relatively high concentration of Reformed Pietist Christians. Nicknamed 'heavy Christians,' these believers tend to have a very self-contained church culture. Alongside this religious population, Sliedrecht has a large group of inhabitants who are totally indifferent - or even hostile - to the church. Finally, the town is home to a significant group of immigrants. We have a Turkish mosque here, for instance. If you go out onto the streets and into the pubs to talk to people in Sliedrecht, you'll find many of them have specific feelings - either positive or negative - about the church. The negative folks may have biases, or they may have experienced real conflicts with(in) the church or be disappointed by it. Others may have left the church out of disinterest. Our aim is to get in touch with all of these people - individuals trying to keep the church at a distance.

---

[3] Pronounce as 'Sleedrecht.'

So who are we? We're a group of about fifty Christians. Around forty of us are involved in youth work at Building 33, and the other ten are involved at COTS. A few of us work in both places.

As far as I know, the Pentecostal church in Sliedrecht prayed actively for a spiritual breakthrough in this town before I came here. God has worked through many people and He is still doing so. Without all those people, this work would never have taken off. My wife, Carolien[4], and I are grateful for the privilege of having become a part of this movement in Sliedrecht.

When I joined the Dutch Reformed Church of Sliedrecht as a pastor on August 22, 1999, the congregation knew I was eager to get the gospel out onto the streets. The church council members were fine with that, and things remained that way until the day of my farewell. It eventually gave rise to some tension, as I wanted to take the congregation to join me in this outward movement. For one thing, it meant our services would have to change, so as to make outsiders feel more comfortable. Some people resisted these changes and irritations arose, becoming public in the spring of 2008. That's when I decided I no longer wanted to pastor a church. But the story that led up to that decision is a long one.

So how did the congregation and I grow apart? My drive to connect with non-church folk has always been there and it was rekindled in Sliedrecht. On Friday evening November 9, 2001, I stepped inside one of the town's pubs for the first time. It may well be that God was showing some humor in using me for this, because my maternal grandparents had owned a pub in the village of Wormer. My grandfather was brought to his knees by God through a pastor visiting the pub after closing time. My mom told me this story. Having been raised in a pub always made her feel she was an inferior Christian.

---

[4] Pronounce as 'Caroleen.'

The appearance of a pastor in the pub was big news in a religious town like Sliedrecht. Most of the folks there were really surprised. A guy with grey hair sitting on a bar stool, even venturing into young people's hangouts - and a pastor, too. Pastors don't do this, do they? I had a lot of great conversations and was often able to pray with people. Later I read in a report on religion issued by Statistics Netherlands (*Religion at the Beginning of the 21st Century*, p. 90) that almost a quarter of Dutch believers prefer not to belong to a church or religious community. Think about it: these people call themselves believers, but they do not want to go to church! It seems likely that in addition to this group there is a large group of seekers as well.

On my visits to the pubs, I discovered that these people really do exist. Seekers! What it is they're seeking, they often don't know themselves. They don't even recognize the inner restlessness that characterizes seekers. In any case, the church in their eyes is a definite no-go. And then there is that other group of individuals who still believe but are fed up with the church. Shortly after my first pub visits, I also attended several conferences. The conferences strengthened my resolve to go out and find these people. At the same time, I experienced an important personal breakthrough, or healing. I began to realize God really wanted me to be alive. It was a new awareness. God wanted me and had a new calling for me. I saw some beautiful things, and the world of charismatic Christianity opened up before my eyes. I knew the reason I was alive was to give people who actually belonged to Jesus a place within a Christian community. During my years in Sliedrecht, there were two periods in which I spent a lot of tears. The first period was when I saw the tremendous need among the sheep of Sliedrecht lacking a shepherd! I sensed the Holy Spirit wanted to renew us, so that those sheep would be reunited with the Shepherd. So I looked for ways of instructing our congregation in the work of the Spirit and opening them up to Him. I also hoped change in this area would transform our services, making them more accessible to seekers. In the fall of 2003, I began to submit my plans to the council. By January 2004, we changed our approach to the afternoon services. A lot of church members were excited, but resistance was growing as well. I hoped the resistance would fade away. My own longings were growing stronger all the time.

2. What is Building 33?

A place where young people can feel at home

I was longing for more, and more started happening! By Pentecost 2004, a prayer movement involving Christians from all kinds of churches and backgrounds was emerging. It was called Miahodos. Our prayers focused on two things: unity among Christians of different backgrounds, and the opportunity to be a blessing to the town of Sliedrecht. Miahodos is Greek for 'one way.' It began impressively. We celebrated Pentecost spending ten evenings in confession, praise and intercession with about seventy-five people. Tears flowed and miracles happened. Next, we set apart one evening every month for praise and prayer. We set up working groups to move beyond prayer, knowing that prayer without obedience is basically a way of misusing the name of God. When God instructed us to pray 'Give us today our daily bread,' He intended for us to take the matter seriously. It means you have to look around for someone to share your bread with, since the prayer is not just for yourself, but for 'our' bread. Similarly, praying for a blessing on Sliedrecht means you have to look around and see whom you can bless. If you don't, you're a hypocrite merely using pious words without meaning.

At one point, I was with a group of people who wanted to do something for the young people of Sliedrecht. An Anglican prophetess once said I had the gift of reaching out to young people, and I had often felt for those young folks hanging around town trying to break free from home - as far as they had one. I'd seen them roaming around Sliedrecht with their big-mouth attitudes and their plastic bags filled with bottles of booze. So I was keen to join in and figure out what we might do for these youngsters. My first thought was: bind up their wounds. Sure, but how…? Nobody really knew. All we could do was trust God to show us the way.

The first dream

He did show us the way, but it was different from what I had expected. The members of the group focused on youth work were hesitant, mainly because of church politics. Nothing happened and after about four meetings we came to the conclusion that it would be better to stop. The youth workers wanted to remain within the comfort of their own church circles. But something had happened inside of me. I had seen a shop building that had been vacant for quite a while. The address was Kerkbuurt 264 (or 264, Church Neighborhood). It was located conveniently near downtown Sliedrecht. The disadvantage was that there was a 'coffee shop' just around the corner - and in the Netherlands the word 'coffee shop' is synonymous to soft drugs. However, the building did not look too expensive - to put it mildly. And every morning as I kneeled down in prayer to prepare myself for a another day, it kept creeping into my prayers. All of this began in the spring of 2005. Morning after morning I would see the building in my mind's eye. It continued on over the summer.

On the morning of Monday, August 22, God led my prayers back to this building once again. And as we noted before, prayer without obedience amounts to misusing His Name. I knew I had to choose: stop praying about the building or take action. But taking action is not something you just get up and do. So I asked God: 'If you really want me to do something with this shop building, give Carolien a dream about a house right now.' Carolien was still in bed. She knew nothing of my obsession with the shop building. When she got up a little while later, the first words we exchanged were pretty normal:

'Good morning, Carolien.'
'Good morning.'
'Slept well?'
'Yeah.'

'Have any dreams?'

I felt kind of nervous.

'Actually, yes, about a house! In fact, there were two: an old place that became new. And I knew how to decorate a room for our son.'

I was amazed! Everything seemed to fit! The shop building really did consist of two buildings: there was the old shop with its living quarters, and the house next door that been added on. As for it being old, anybody could see that. I was beside myself with excitement. 'Carolien, write down every detail of that dream!' Baffled by my behavior, she asked, 'Why?' 'I'll tell you later, just write it down!' As soon as I felt most normal people would be up and about, I called a friend who I figured would know a thing or two about home appraisal. I needed him to come over right away and give me some advice. Obediently, he came as quickly as he could. I told him I was planning on buying the property.

Carolien heard me sharing my excitement and replied in her usual down-to-earth manner, 'How do you plan to buy it?'

I had no idea, of course. So I mumbled something about sending out a mailing to wealthy Christians; that was sure to work. Carolien was quick to knock down my foolish financing proposal. 'We have to buy it ourselves,' she said. And then she added, smiling, 'This is not my idea, it's from God.'

She then went on to share that for some time she had felt God asking her to let go of the vicarage we had been living in. She had met people at Youth With A Mission who had given up everything and willingly embraced a very simple lifestyle in order to be completely available for God's service. From the moment she had met these people, a small voice in her heart had begun to challenge her, 'Carolien, do you have the courage to leave everything behind? Could you leave your comfortable vicarage for a ruin?' Carolien suggested we use the rent we paid for the vicarage to get a mortgage on the shop building. She was also convinced it would be unwise to purchase a building and have several different people run it; it would be better for us to manage it ourselves. For the second time that morning, I was amazed - this time, by Carolien's wisdom! She's usually a wise person, but right then she was clearly being guided by God in what she said.

Financial resources

The building badly needed renovating, but we did not have the financial means for that. Neither did we know where to get the number of people we would need to get the job done. But it all worked out. We bought a building all but in ruins. A civil engineer kindly evaluated the whole construction for us. I remember him groaning and sighing as he walked from one room to the next. I was more aware than ever that getting this place shipshape would take a true miracle. He recommended installing a steel arch to support a part of the building that was showing signs of sinking into the ground; without the arch, he said, the whole building might collapse - the building in which we were to live and set up a youth ministry.

We wondered what we'd gotten ourselves into, but at the same time we knew that God would show us the way forward - we'd seen too much already to doubt that. Financially, for instance, it almost seemed as if God was forcing us to push ahead. Even before we had signed the purchase contract, our story had had so much press coverage that we couldn't possibly back out. We signed the contract on Friday, October 28, 2005. After that we took off for a weekend out of town with our kids. Carolien was hoping that over the weekend some money would come in from somewhere. But nothing happened! She couldn't sleep that Monday night. She prayed, she wracked her brain, she worried, she prayed some more... 'How is this ever going to work?' She realized we could start asking for gifts, at least to cover the part of the building we wanted to use for youth work. We had already set up a foundation for that purpose. But our living quarters were a mess as well. Everything was crooked and the whole place looked neglected and unattractive. Where would we get the money to fix it up? Our own funds had all gone into the mortgage!

After that sleepless night, Carolien received a phone call from a lady who said she felt she had to do something. She pledged to give 20,000 euros for our private living quarters. Carolien was overjoyed! That same day she bumped into a guy who was involved in the renovation. She immediately started telling him about the 20,000 euro miracle.

'So how much do you think we'll need to get our living quarters completely fixed up?' she asked him.

He stopped to think for a minute. 'I'd say at least 30,000 euros!'

'That's wonderful! We already have 20,000!'

Not long after that, there was another phone call. 'Carolien, I'd like to donate 10,000 euros.'

Thank you, thank you, thank you! That's how God works! But we weren't there yet. We knew we were not just in need of funds for our own home, but also for the youth center. Carolien felt I should call a certain businessman. I'd mentioned him several times, but had never had the courage to call. So maybe I should. I wouldn't be calling out of selfish motives, after all, but for God's work.

I called him. He was busy and didn't give me a lot of time to share my plans; instead, he told me to call back the next day. In the meantime, he told me later, he went down on his knees and asked God for clarity as to what to do and how much to contribute. He prayed for a sign: if I asked him for 10,000 euros, he would know it was the right thing to do. I called. Again, his response was curt. No nonsense. 'How much do you want?'

'Huh? Um... well, actually I need 10,000 euros.' I still can't believe I was foolish enough to ask for an amount like that, but I did and an hour later it had been transferred to our foundation's bank account.

By now we were ready to prepare for the move to 264, Kerkbuurt. The vicarage would soon be a thing of the past - a fact that caused a lot of consternation in the church! 'The pastor has such weird ideas, and now this? What does he think he's doing? Now we won't be able to use our beautiful vicarage for what it's intended for! And what about the church budget? The vicarage won't bring in any money if it doesn't have any tenants! And if our pastor is going to work with those kids that hang around in the streets, how will he manage to take proper care of the congregation?'

A tough church meeting followed. There were objections, questions, letters... How could the church council allow this to happen? The council tried to explain things as best as it could. As for the finances, they didn't know how things would work out either.

But God did know. The weekend after the church meeting, everything had been sorted out. Out of nowhere, a potential tenant had turned up. He was in a hurry, too, and what's more - he would be paying more than *we* had for the vicarage!

Everything fell into place. The new tenant needed the vicarage by June, which meant the pastor would need help vacating the vicarage - and quickly, too. Suddenly, the people who had grumbled the loudest were helping us move house, and on June 3, 2006, we moved into our new home.

The logo of Building 33 ('Pand' in Dutch - pronounce as 'wand'). Look carefully, and you'll see the number 33 (two threes placed back to back) as well as the shapes of a heart, an anchor and the cross.

Soon we were ready for Phase 2 of the renovation: the part of the building we wanted to use for youth work. Many of the loyal folk who had helped us in the beginning were tired now and backed out. For weeks on end, nothing happened. Our home was cold and damp. We didn't have any heating yet, and winter was approaching. Our faith was being put to the test again. Thank God, new workers turned up and we were able to complete the renovation of Building 33.

The name

We chose the name 'Building 33,' as it has (at least in the Dutch language) a tough kind of ring to it, while the number 33 is a reference to how old Jesus was when He was crucified and raised from the dead, and the Spirit was poured out. It was now 2007. On March 3, at 3 minutes past 3 in the afternoon, Building 33 was officially opened. Carolien, anticipating a busy time for us, had resigned from her job as a social worker with the Salvation Army. We weren't sure whether we'd be able to make ends meet, but, again, God did not let us down. We definitely needed some extra support from Him, because the opening of Building 33 marked the beginning of an extremely demanding period of our lives.

A neighborhood in upheaval

Our neighbors soon threatened to take legal action. And they did. Some wanted indemnification for this, that and the other. The fact that Building 33 met with this kind of resistance was understandable. Its opening had turned the neighborhood upside down. In the early days, there were often over a hundred young people hanging out in the former shop. The sidewalks were black with bicycles: ten yards of sidewalk in front of the neighbor's home and another twelve yards right in front of Building 33 - black with bicycles. One very disgruntled neighbor came and told us that one of our young people had decided to take a walk all over his Mercedes - without bothering to erase his tracks. It was not a great way for us to get to know our new neighborhood.

In those days, we naively believed it would be okay for us to keep Building 33 open until 2 am on Fridays and Saturdays. On Thursdays and Sundays, we figured, we could close down earlier, but on Fridays and Saturdays we wanted to keep young people away from the bars, which meant staying open until the early hours of the morning. What well-meaning fools we were... You see, we thought the young folk would be good little boys and girls and spend the entire evening at our place without drinking a drop of alcohol, because we didn't serve any. We still don't, as a matter of fact, but we soon lost our naivety as to the relationships between young people, alcohol and cannabis. In this field, young people are very creative and very inventive. Building 33 really is a great place: with its rough woodwork and furniture and its warm colors, it exudes a pleasant, homy atmosphere. The whole setup, in fact, was a huge success right from the start - but not as an alcohol-free zone...

The problem was that large amounts of chemical substances were carried right into our building in the stomachs, veins and lungs of our young guests. In no time, our street was totally transformed. Young folk would show up way past the middle of the night to drop in at the 'coziest venue' in Sliedrecht. So what if they didn't sell alcoholic beverages there - filling up on cheap booze out in the street was completely normal to these kids. And now Building 33 offered them the luxury of chilling out on a comfy sofa and even doing some gaming, shooting some pool or trying the X-box if you still had the energy. There was plenty of fun to be had in Building 33! And if you got thirsty, well, all you had to do was step outside, find the booze you stashed away behind a hedge or around a corner and empty another half or whole bottle before noisily staggering back to Building 33!

It's no wonder the neighborhood was not amused by these Christian idealists. At night they were kept awake by all the yelling, and during the day they would find traces of loose living in their front yards. And when they ventured out into the street themselves, they were afraid they'd run into aggressive youngsters.

The police, the mayor and local politicians all showed up to discuss the problem of Building 33. A storm had risen and it was getting worse. One evening it swept right into Building 33 itself, with some youngsters getting into a fist fight - I had to chase one hundred young people right out onto the street. Everybody out!

Our plan didn't seem to be working. After a month of de-stressing, we decided to try another tack. We wanted to get to know young folk personally and if they came in one hundred at a time, building personal relationships was impossible. First, we introduced a pass system, offering the two main groups of youngsters separate access to Building 33 two afternoons and evenings a week. This helped a lot in restoring the peace. Now we were open four days a week, with only one group coming at a time.

Our aim was to bind up the wounds of the young people, but unintentionally we had turned the neighborhood into one big sore. After we changed course, the sore got better, and gradually the neighborhood began to appreciate our work. Some folk needed a little more time to recover, but eventually they did, too. What may have helped is that folks could see we were not exclusively focused on young people: we tried to help all kinds of people who had somehow run into difficulties. This is how COTS, the acronym for Church on the Street, came into being. We wanted to be a blessing to seekers and to anybody else who felt stuck. But as this vision developed, new problems arose with our church council.

3. What is COTS?

Searching for the unorganized church

In those days I carried on visiting pubs and bars. Meanwhile, I doubled my efforts to keep giving the congregation what it is entitled to. But the grumbling didn't stop and I felt the church was falling short of its call to minister to the world. We were growing apart at an alarming rate. Looking back, I have to say I did not recognize what was happening. There were so many opportunities out on the street! So many great contacts, so many seekers - surely, we had to do something for them! I felt I was being called to serve these people. But some people in our congregation resisted my drive. This became evident during a council meeting on June 4, 2008. I was not there, but when I read the minutes later, I knew I had just lost an illusion: I couldn't go on like this! I told the council that I was no longer sure I should continue as a pastor, and they replied that they, too, were having difficulties working with me.

In the first chapter, I mentioned I have gone through two periods of tears. This church council meeting marked the beginning of the second one. For months on end, I felt intensely sorrowful. I had the feeling my labor in Sliedrecht had been for nothing. I was being forced to quit! The worst thing about it was that some members of the congregation were glad I was about to leave. It all seemed like one giant failure. Carolien started sharing passages of Scripture with me that she had received during her prayer times. She knows the Bible well, but can't always remember the exact Bible references. So when she receives a text, she has no idea how it came to her. She had seen my months of sadness. On August 21, she set apart some time to pray. During that time, she received two texts. The first one was about unconditional obedience, and the second about the purpose of this obedience. Scripture verse number one was from Matthew

8:9: 'For I am a man under authority, having soldiers under me: and I say to this man, Go, and he goeth; and to another, Come, and he cometh; and to my servant, Do this, and he doeth it.' It was as if God was saying to me, 'Gerard, stop whining and get going!' The second Scripture was from Matthew 10:6: 'But go rather to the lost sheep of the house of Israel.' It fit right into what I had been praying all along. Both of these verses from the Bible were really instrumental in helping me accept the new situation.

The second dream

But something else had happened. On January 9, some six months before this crisis occurred, the pastor of the Pentecostal church in Sliedrecht had e-mailed me, sharing a dream he'd had. His dream now turned out to have been prophetic. In his dream, he had seen me standing in the back of our church building, overcome with sorrow - until an opening appeared at the back of the building. It was like a breach in the wall. Looking through it, I had seen a miraculous fruit tree outside the church building: it was a tree loaded with tomatoes. Tomatoes don't grow on trees! God was revealing that I must seek certain kinds of fruit in unexpected places.

Only later did I understand this dream as a pointer towards looking for fruit beyond our church. There was something else about the dream. At the top of the tree, there was this silver tomato. Since silver in the Old Testament tabernacle usually had a strong supportive function, I took the silver tomato to mean that one day that tree would bring forth a church capable of supporting its members. On September 3, 2008, I shared my final decision with the church council. We agreed to take out one year for the transition. Meanwhile, I got busy looking for another job. With a little extra income and a gift here and there, we figured we might make it. Added to the financial insecurity we were facing, there were also tensions about my position in the church. Since I had handed in my resignation, it was not likely I would remain a reverend: quitting is paramount to disqualifying yourself. Thankfully, some colleagues stood up for me at this time. They spoke with our church council and other church bodies, requesting that I remain a reverend. On July 1, 2009, my years as an active pastor of the Sliedrecht church were over. I was classified as a retired pastor, but without the financial benefits. Meanwhile, on the job hunting front, I had no leads at all. No matter how hard I tried, I just couldn't find a suitable job anywhere. Not that I needed one, as God was providing for us - and pretty well, too! Month after month, enough money came in for us to live on. A new journey had begun. The ministry grew rapidly. Carolien and I understood that God was providing for us so well, because He wanted to free us up for the job He had given us to do. Together we formed a new legal partnership, COTS. The word church, by the way, is derived from the Greek word 'kuriakè,' which means: that which belongs to the Lord. We liked that. We go out searching for people who live their lives outside the organized church, but do belong to the Lord. We recognized that God has an unorganized church and we want to try and connect with the Spirit's movements in that church. Carolien covers the social side, and I'm responsible for the missionary and pastoral aspects. Together with a great team of co-workers, we are witnessing an amazing development.

The logo of 'Church on the Street,' COTS for short. The power of the cross and the resurrection is breaking through on the streets and in pubs.

What we do

So what is it we actually do? Every first Sunday of the month, we have a morning service at a local pub. These services are usually attended by a regular group of pub customers, a varying group of people simply interested in finding out what it's all about, and a small number of co-workers. The average attendance is around 60.

Also, we publish monthly articles in a local paper on our 'church in the pub.' The articles typically center on people and their faith. They're very well read throughout Sliedrecht. A lot of readers are surprised to find faith in people they would never have considered believers. The same paper also publishes a pub church service announcement every month - free of charge.

All other Sundays, when there is no 'pub service,' we have services at Building 33. These start at 5 pm and involve a lot of talking, praying, singing, food and fellowship. About 25 people usually turn up. We often use movies about the Bible. Some of our participants hardly know anything about the Bible, and movies are an easy way for them to get acquainted with it. But these meetings have plenty of depth, too. We try to be really honest with each other, sharing things that might withhold us from surrendering to God and exploring how God works in these areas. We learn from each other. Every one of us has his or her own history. Some have struggled with addiction, others have had other problems. Several people attending these get-togethers have come to the Lord. Others have joined us because they were unable to settle in a regular church or, for reasons of their own, have turned their backs on the church. Several of our co-workers also participate, offering pastoral and practical support.

Every other Wednesday, we have another group, only this one is smaller and we don't have meals together. The composition of this group is different; it attracts a different set of people. Currently, about fifteen folks attend, including a few of our co-workers. Attendance here varies a little more than it does on Sundays.

We also have a regular group of eight to ten young people from Building 33 come over every two weeks for French fries and conversation. We're always looking for new ways of communicating with young people. Flexibility is a key word.

Another group of five people has emerged as well. I got to know them at a local youth center known for the large amounts of marijuana and alcohol that are used there. Many of its regular visitors are in their thirties and struggling with various forms of addiction. The five I now run a discussion group with every two weeks consider themselves believers. We can see them gradually changing. The meetings are held in participants' homes.

For another group of seven or eight folks, we have found an apartment we can use for get-togethers. They feel comfortable there. It was made available to us for offering shelter and support to people threatened with ending up on the streets. It can take two people.

For jobs that need doing, there is a group of volunteers I can call on. At COTS, we also have someone who can help folks fill out their tax forms. These are typical examples of how we are constantly looking for practical ways of helping people. Another one is a garage we have, where we store discarded furniture and household items and give them to people who don't have the money to buy these things themselves.

We have a professional movie camera, an experienced cameraman and an interviewer. This little team goes out onto the streets to do interviews on topics related to church and the world. We've also been to the mosque for interviews with Muslims. It's a great way of starting a conversation about our faith. Some of these interviews are broadcast on regional TV.

Then we have a discipleship school, where we train people to use their gifts in God's Kingdom. About ten to fifteen people follow the program every year.

Another of our groups is for people with a handicap. This group meets once a month. We enjoy food, have lots of fun and great conversations together.

Our building is also used by other local churches, for Alpha courses, for instance. Some groups use our facilities for meetings, as it is a comfortable, pleasant place to get together.

Building 33 is open for young people on Thursday afternoons and evenings, Saturday afternoons and evenings, and Sunday afternoons. We have about ninety different kids dropping in on a weekly basis. We're also involved in a youth network that deals with kids who are stuck in one way or another. The police regularly contacts us to discuss bottlenecks or to request counseling and support for troubled youths. We have about a hundred addresses of people we visit from time to time or who call on us now and again because of problems.

I go out to the bars and pubs at least two nights a week to make contact with people. It almost always leads to meaningful conversations. It's not uncommon for me to end up praying with someone at a bar. Occasionally I drop in during the daytime, as there are different people around then.

All of these experiences have gradually changed my perspective on evangelism. I would really love for us Christians to go out into the world in a new way. It would be so great if we could learn to really connect with what God is doing in people's lives. It would be wonderful if in doing this we could find new openings that would enable those other people to discover the loving kindness of God, who is the Giver of all good gifts.

A vision of evangelism centered on connecting (Chapters 4-12)

In Chapters 4 through 12, I'd like to show you why I believe the kind of feverish evangelism we often see is actually counterproductive. I believe a more pastoral approach is far more in line with the example Jesus gave us and with what we read in the Book of Acts. We have to learn to connect with what God's Spirit is doing or has done in the lives of other people. In this section, I'd also like to discuss the grounds for this approach.

4. What do you mean, 'Stop the fever and learn to connect?'

A different perspective on evangelism

'You know what really annoys me about you people? That we accept you, but you never accept us!'

This guy was right! I was sitting next to him at a bar; a friend of his was sitting on his other side. They were both in their thirties, and their eyelids and cheeks were drooping from all the alcohol and drugs running through their veins. But the young man speaking to me still had the clarity of mind to react as if he'd just been stung.

At first he had not shown much interest, but when he heard I was a pastor, it took him a couple of seconds to overcome the shock. Then he asked a few questions just to make sure his ears weren't playing tricks on him: 'Are you serious? A pastor?' I could read his mind, 'Another one of those Christians. What's this guy doing here?'

It meant he had met other members of my spiritual family and not particularly enjoyed the encounter! Then he swung me that knock-out punch, 'What really annoys me about you people is that we accept you, but you never accept us!'

Sadly, I instantly knew what he meant. Every time he met some member of my spiritual family, he was told, be it sometimes implicitly, that he had to change. He didn't believe in God and they did, right? They were right, he was wrong. They were the goodies, he was a baddie. They went to church every Sunday, he never did. They were converted and had God. He didn't know what they were talking about. Sure, he was willing to accept they had something special. He was even prepared to treat them like normal people - but time and again it just didn't work. At every encounter with a Christian, this unbridgeable gap would appear - and the only way of bridging it was for him to change. Which, of course, he refused.

This fellow is one more victim of well-meaning brothers and sisters of mine suffering from evangelistic fever and a kind of professional blindness. Sometimes their approach works; they apply the right amount of tact and love, and something good happens. But all too often, these Christians are completely insensitive to the loathing their approach causes. In the reaction of the young man I was talking to, it was pretty evident - and I'm sad to say I've come across this type of reaction, in one form or another, many, many times. And every time it shocks me to hear folk tell me how they've been attacked by my own dear family members, Christians intent on saving people who have no desire whatsoever to be saved. I know my family members are driven by love. I know God values this love more highly than anything in this world. So who am I to comment? They may have a greater love than I do. I know my failures and shortcomings. Maybe I'm all wrong and their radical approach is the better of the two. Maybe we should take the loathing for granted. Maybe... but I don't think so. I honestly believe these Christians are behaving kind of neurotically.

Street work means connecting

Initially, I considered the title *Stop the evangelism fever* for this book. The idea was for it to be a wake-up call, an appeal to Christians to stop being so feverish about evangelism. Somebody graciously suggested a title like that would not easily be recognized by readers, so I dropped it. But I still hope that together we will develop new approaches to evangelism, avoiding the minefield that explodes into a moralism at every touch. Let's stop being so feverish and restless about it. Fever is a sign of ill health. It's not a good thing and I can't imagine it pleases God, even if He sees the love behind it. Blind love has led to many errors. Is there a different way? Yes. Is it better? We'll have to find out.

The subtitle to this book is short and offers a cure for the fever of evangelism: street work means connecting. I deliberately avoided the use of the word evangelism in choosing this title, because in my view evangelism is just another form of pastoral care. In the Dutch version, I've centered on the word 'verbinden,' which has two meanings: it can refer to the binding up of wounds, but it can also mean 'to connect,' 'to get in touch' or 'to become bound up with.' To me, the two meanings are closely related: only in truly connecting to people can we begin to help them bind up their wounds.

There are many different kinds of wounds; in the course of our lives, we can get hurt in lots of ways, and all those injuries need attention. There are physical wounds, psychological wounds, spiritual wounds. Even material losses can qualify as wounds. Binding up these wounds is the work of the Good Samaritan. He was a blessing to the wounded victim he bumped into along the way. So binding up wounds is synonymous to blessing. It's about doing a specific good deed for someone, so that he or she will experience the blessing of God's Kingdom at the hands of our spiritual family. Our Brother Jesus taught us this when He spoke about our Father:

'(...) for He maketh His sun to rise on the evil and on the good, and sendeth rain on the just and the unjust' (Matt. 5:45).

Then there's that other meaning of the Dutch word 'verbinden': connecting, or becoming 'bound up,' with something or someone. To me, this is about connecting with all that is of God. Everything that comes from God is beautiful and good, and we must learn to recognize it in creation, but certainly also in the people around us - even people we might consider 'unjust.' Especially in them! Only then will we be able to honor our Father for all the goodness we encounter. It takes practice, but as we progress we learn to freely go out into the world and to identify and name all that is of God. He's entitled to it!

So there are two forms of 'binding':

1. Becoming bound up with other people in relationships, or connecting with people by connecting with the blessing God has given them.
2. Binding up wounds by being a blessing to others in need of binding up in any way that offers those persons blessing and healing.

Starting in Chapter 13, we will look at 'how it works.' What are our options for finding new ways of binding up and becoming bound up? I just want to make sure you understand what I mean when I'm using that word, 'verbinden,' or binding. What effects do I see resulting from all this?

Binding up wounds and becoming bound up with people, I believe, works like this:

a. You show the other person you want to connect with him by being willing to recognize God's work in his life or by beginning to bind up his wounds.

b. That person begins to appreciate your interest and in turn shows you that he wants to connect with you.
c. You look for ways of expressing your connectedness.
d. The other person begins to show an interest in your faith and opens up to it.
e. A change occurs that is known as conversion.

These things mark the beginning of a pastoral journey. Usually, a journey of this type requires a lot of patience - certainly when you're working out on the streets. But before we go into more detail, I'd like to explain why I like to call myself a 'street pastor.'

5. Why a street pastor and not an evangelist?

A brief study of the New Testament evangelist

Let me explain why I do not use the term 'evangelist' to describe my work. Then you'll automatically see why I call myself a 'street pastor.' Others may choose to stick with the term evangelist, which, of course, is fine - but if this chapter helps them in becoming a little more pastorally oriented, I'll consider that a gain. Obviously, the term 'evangelist' has certain advantages, as many folk will recognize it. Usually, people think of an evangelist as someone whose job it is to turn unbelievers into believers. The drawback, of course, is that evangelism is associated with a certain kind of behavior people tend to resist.

Evangelist

The word evangelist in our day has lost some of the richness and breadth of meaning it had in New Testament times. An evangelist in the New Testament did not just go around talking about the good news; he demonstrated the reality of it. He didn't just use his vocal cords, but he made manifest the power of this good news. That explains why Paul wrote that 'the kingdom of God is not in word, but in power' (1 Cor. 4:20).

The word 'evangelist' is derived from the Greek word 'euangelistès,' which means proclaimer of glad tidings. But an evangelist also set things in motion, as God Himself was at work in the words spoken. The angel Gabriel brought good news to Zechariah in the temple (Luke 1:19) and the angel of the Lord also appeared to the shepherds in the field to bring 'good tidings of great joy' (Luke 2:10). In the same vein, John the Baptist was an evangelist (Luke 3:18). He announced the dawn of a new era and moved people to get ready for it. It's evident that an evangelist in the biblical sense did a lot more than just announcing the news. His proclamations were accompanied by the actual unfolding of the events he spoke of.

In New Testament times, the birth of an emperor was commonly announced in public. After that, his coming of age would be announced, and later his accession to the throne. These announcements were made by a 'bringer of good news' (euangelistès). This good news was accompanied by actions. Sacrifices were brought, gifts given and celebrations held - all to emphasize that the things proclaimed had actually entered into force. (See *Theological Dictionary*, by Geoffrey W. Bromiley, p. 267 ff.)

It is fair to say Jesus is the ultimate Evangelist. He was even more than that. He did not only proclaim the good news, He *was* the good news. He set the good news in motion by demonstrating the power of the Kingdom in the form of blessings showered on the people. He said, 'the same works that I do, bear witness of Me, that the Father hath sent Me.' (John 5:36). This is significant. It is exactly why Jesus sent out His disciples with the authority to wield the power of the Kingdom as evidence of its coming (Matt. 10:1; Mark 16:17-18).[5] So if you want to do the work of an evangelist in a scriptural way, it must involve a release of power and blessings to be freely bestowed on the people. Jesus did just that. This doesn't mean everyone got converted (Matt. 11:20). He gave freely, just as His Father did. Looking at God the Father, we see first the blessing of His reign (sun, rain and fruitfulness - Matt. 5:45); He calls on us to recognize Him as the Giver (Is. 1:1-3; John 1:4-6; Rom. 1:20). We tend to start with the words, forgetting the New Testament model, which says: demonstrate the reality of the things you proclaim. In other words, demonstrate the power of God's Kingdom. We often talk randomly about God, doing the very thing Jesus

---

[5] Mark 16:17-18. Even if this section was inserted into the text later, as some suggest, the perspective it offers on evangelism evidently remained unchanged.

told us not to, the things fools do: fools cast their pearls before swine (Matt. 7:6). Swine like to eat moldy bread. Feed them pearls and they'll turn on you! On the street, we don't always know who we're dealing with. Some people really are like swine - they will never appreciate the beauty or the value of a pearl, simply because it is not destined for them (1 Pet. 2:8). Sometimes there is initial resistance, because people are not yet ready (Gal. 1:13-24). The words of the gospel are words of power. If a person is not ready, we must not provoke him; instead, we should wait until he is ready.

At one point, someone else in our town wanted to start evangelizing. So what did he do? He scrawled the good news on a wall at one of the favorite hangouts of some street kids. The kids had just repainted the place themselves. But our evangelist must have thought to himself, 'Okay, I'm going to spray-paint a great text on that wall.' These are the words he sprayed: 'Only Jesus brings happiness!' I heard the guys grumbling about this 'evangelist' one time when they were hanging out in Building 33. The spray-painted message about Jesus did not bring them any happiness at all!

A co-worker at Building 33 made the same mistake. Some guys were sitting downstairs watching their favorite TV show. Our guy, no doubt thinking he was doing something really meaningful, turned on some praise music and turned it up loud on the speakers downstairs - and those things produce a lot of volume. The response from downstairs was predictable: 'Hey, you Christian idiots, turn off that music!'

Noticeable blessings

Let's sum things up by saying that the task of an evangelist as presented in the New Testament involves not only words, but tangible blessings accompanying those words - blessings freely shared with everyone. That's what happened in Malta. We don't read about any conversions there, all we read is that Paul and his co-workers were honored (Acts 28:9-10). Pay attention here, because this is a great example! Acts of blessing preceded words and conversions. It may well be that nobody got converted in Malta! Paul was known as an apostle, but also as an evangelist - as were many others (Rom. 10:15).

It seems likely that the people referred to as evangelists were engaged in all kinds of work. In Acts 6, for example, we read that Philip helped to ease the burden of the apostles, enabling them to focus on their core business within the church. But we also see Philip doing the work of an evangelist. He is the only one explicitly referred to as 'the evangelist' (Acts 21:8), and the characteristics of an evangelist are all there. In Samaria, his preaching was accompanied by the healing of the lame and the crippled. Unclean spirits were cast out there as well (Acts 8). Following his encounter with the Ethiopian 'eunuch of great authority' and the man's baptism, a miraculous change occurred. And let's not forget the miraculous way in which Philip met the Ethiopian and how he disappeared from the scene after their exchange… This was evangelism accompanied by unusual power!

Timothy was also called to do the work of an evangelist (2 Tim. 4:5). We know that for a long time he led the church in Ephesus. Looking at him from the perspective of what we now know about an evangelist, we can see some recognizable things in his ministry. His message was accompanied by power (1 Thess. 3:2). People suffering severe persecution received power from God through Timothy's ministry - to the extent that their faith and love remained standing throughout their trials (1 Thess. 3:6).

The fact that the authors of the gospels are also referred to as 'evangelists' may have to do with the fact that they, too, had an active part in spreading the blessings of God's Kingdom. Their writings were in themselves a powerful blessing. But there is no doubt that their ministry of words was accompanied by the evidence of deeds. We know Mark was right behind Peter and Paul in their work. Luke was another of Paul's co-workers, helping him to share God's loving kindness. The apostles Matthew and John are equally known for spreading God's blessings wherever they went.

I have no doubt that in our day and age there are many people doing what the Bible characters we've just looked at were doing - combining a ministry of the word with the evidence of deeds. These people, as far as I am concerned, have every right to call themselves evangelists. But I no longer feel comfortable with the word 'evangelist,' because in the past it has so often been used in the limited sense of Christians bluntly confronting non-believers with the good news, without the least awareness of the resistance they were raising. As if the good news of the gospel has to be pushed down people's throats. To me, the combination of a ministry of words and the performance of works that confirm those words makes much more sense - and usually in the reverse order!

Without force

All of this does raise questions. Are we not instructed, after all, to preach the Word constantly, 'be instant in season, out of season,' urging people to listen? Paul told Timothy to adopt a firm attitude, didn't he? (2 Tim. 4:2) Try arguing with that! Other sections of the New Testament may give the same impression: that we're supposed to put some muscle into spreading the gospel. Jesus seems to suggest it in one of His parables: '(...) compel them to come in,' He said (Luke 14:23).

Let's pick up on that last statement first. The word translated as 'compel' carries the meaning of the word 'persuade.' It means we must show people the urgency of the matter and prove to them that it makes sense. That is the kind of 'compelling' we are called to. It's like giving people a little prod. The parable it is used in is about a rich man throwing a big party. You get the feeling he is a local celebrity. If you can throw a party like that, you're obviously in the picture. But the invitees didn't want to come. Now this man was not about to let his party get ruined by the indifference of his network. So he decided to invite a different set of people! '(...) go out quickly into the streets and lanes of the city, and bring in hither the poor, and the maimed, and the halt, and the blind,' he said to his servant (v. 21). The poor folk in town were excited about attending the party, because they all knew the man giving it. But still there were empty seats, there was room for more guests. So he said to his servant, '(...) go out into the highways and hedges' (v. 23). This meant going beyond the familiar streets of the town into unknown territory. People out there did not know the man. They needed some convincing that it was really alright to go the party of some unknown do-gooder. You see, this story is not about nagging and forcing people to do something they don't want to do. It's about earnestly addressing them and encouraging them to overcome their doubts.

With Timothy, it was different. He worked in Ephesus. And we know that for a minister of the Word, Ephesus was a tough place to be. The believers there were about to backslide so badly they would need a warning from Christ Himself. The candlestick of the Word was at risk of being removed from their midst! Their love was growing weak (Acts 20:29-30; Rev. 2:4-5). Paul showed Timothy how this downfall was already happening. A day would come when people would no longer put up with sound doctrine. Instead, they would follow their own lusts, to be 'turned unto fables' (2 Tim. 4:3-4 - see also 3:1-9). In his first letter to Timothy, Paul had already warned against these evil forces at work in Ephesus (1 Tim. 1:19; 6:20-21). He told Timothy to find faithful men and to train them as teachers (2 Tim. 2:2). So this was a time of emergency - a time of trying to salvage what could be salvaged. And in this situation, Timothy was urged to seize every opportunity to warn the Ephesians, 'in season, out of season.' The texts in Luke 14 and 2 Timothy 4 offer no ground for forcing the gospel down people's throats.

Jesus' approach is very different. Whenever He noticed that the hearts of His listeners were not open to what He had to say (Matt. 13:15), He started to speak in riddles. He used parables - not to clarify His message, but to find out who was interested enough to actually draw near. If a person came to Him to ask what the parable meant, He knew that person was receptive to the secrets of the Kingdom (Matt. 13:10-13), and was more than willing to explain. He knew this approach meant that to some of His listeners the message would remain hidden. It was a deliberate choice. Jesus was seeking those worthy of receiving the riches of the gospel (Matt. 10:37-39). If people wanted to walk away, He let them (John 6:66-67).

Street pastor

So why do I prefer to use the word 'street pastor,' or 'street counselor?' Because in our day and age the word 'evangelist' has been cut loose from its New Testament connotations of acts of mercy and sensitivity to those worthy of hearing. To me, the concept of pastoral care is much easier to align with things like listening, building relationships and caring. The term 'street pastor' fits into a lifelong pastoral process - something I will get back to later in this book.

I was greatly inspired by reading a description offered by L. Praamsma in *The Church of the Ages* (Dutch: *De kerk van alle tijden*, part 1, pp. 30-32) of how Christianity grew in the first few centuries as a result of pastoral care. Here are some characteristics he mentions:

1. Early Christians were known for their sacrificial lifestyles, with even the poorest among them giving alms.
2. They took care of their spiritual leaders.

3. They supported widows and orphans - not just those within their own community, but also those of non-believing families.
4. They took care of the sick, the weak and of invalids and founded hospitals.
5. They took care of prisoners and mine workers.
6. They arranged funerals for the poor and looked after the dead.
7. They took care of slaves.
8. They provided for people in disaster areas.
9. They labored to ensure that everyone could work for his or her own living (job creation).
10. They helped travelers on their way by giving them money.

Because of these various expressions of pastoral care, the church of those days grew explosively. Pastoral care, then, centers on establishing a deep sense of connection. To illustrate the importance of connecting in my understanding of our work, in the next chapter I'd like to share with you the story of Robert.

6. How do you get connected with people?

By seeing what God is doing in the other person's life and tapping into that

I had seen Robert before during some of my night-time outings to the bars and pubs. He was a disk jockey in a bar in which I felt kind of unwelcome. The regular customers would sit there lurking at me from drooping eyes as if I was the greatest slob they'd ever seen. I could see their mouths mumbling in between sips of drink. I was someone they wanted to keep at a distance. And it seemed to me that Robert felt the same way.

It wasn't until sometime later that I found out how wrong I had been about his character. Unfortunately, that happens quite a lot. Actually, some complications occurred in this particular bar. Robert had been told I was really bad and that Christians are a set of people you need to watch out for anyway, because they're usually hypocrites. I think that was roughly his perception of me. He'd heard stuff about me and it had made him pretty angry. So one day he came barging into Building 33.

'Where is the pastor? I need to talk to the pastor!'

His long hair hung about his head in a wild mess and he was scanning the room as if in search of prey. The other young folk in Building 33 quieted down and stood or sat watching in silence. It turned out Robert had heard we served alcohol at our center and he was intent on finding out for himself. Allowing minors to drink alcohol - just think! It sounded just like something a pastor would do!

His entry gave Carolien and me a fright. We tried to be friendly, but, of course, it didn't help much under the circumstances. Eventually, we got Robert to come with us to our private living quarters. I complimented him for coming and asked him how he would feel if I went around spreading lies about him that I'd picked up somewhere without finding out if they were true.

'Of course I'd be annoyed,' he said.

That was my first toehold in the conversation. After that, we went and showed him around the center. He saw the kids having fun and enjoying themselves. He knew what they were like out on the streets, and yet here they were playing games together! His perception changed radically and from that day on he became a staunch defender of Building 33.

See God's love in the other person

A couple of years later, Robert came round to see me again. He was organizing a charity campaign at his bar. If you want to get things done, you call on your friends, right? Actually, Robert was raising funds for kids with cancer and he wanted to organize a fundraiser concert, too - at his bar. Part of the profit made by the bar would be donated to the cancer fund. Naturally, Robert assumed I'd be eager to support him. His eyes shone as he told me about his project. He's such a beautiful person when his compassion starts shining through! Robert was so thankful for his own good health, especially as quite a few people in his surroundings were ill. The thought of young children facing the horrors of cancer was almost too much for him.

I clapped him on the shoulder and said, 'You know, Robert, I can see a glimmer of God's love in you!'

That confused Robert. I mean, sure, he could believe there was some greater power out there - but the idea that God might be at work in him was just, well - it was the very last thing he would ever have thought of! It made him feel a little unsure of himself, but kind of pleased, too.

You know what was going on at that moment? A connection was being made: God was doing something in Robert and I had recognized it as coming from God. God was establishing a relationship. There we stood: Gerard the pastor and Robert the disk jockey from that bar that seemed so hostile to God - suddenly connected by God's work!

Needless to say I gave Robert's campaign all the support I could. It was a way of becoming bound up in something good. Mind you, I didn't connect with every aspect of the event. I kept a distance from the booze fest the campaign involved at Robert's bar. But I did a lot of talking with the people who joined in. And I always believe that will have an effect. If one of these guys dies, I go to the funeral or cremation. I drop in at the gym to watch the fellows do their boxing workout. I don't attach myself to everything they attach themselves to, but I try to connect with what God is doing in the lives of these individuals. Which means that wherever they are, I need to be, too! That's how relationships start growing and changing! I've seen changes of this nature taking place in the lead singer of a popular local band. Or in two scantily clad female bar favorites - who one day surprised me by asking me to pray for a man on drugs. It turned out one of those women was his wife, and she and her friend were really worried. I connected with that. It was the work of God in that lady's heart. This is how to bridge the gap caused by sin in order to really reach that other person. Robert often attends our church services at the Korevaar pub nowadays. He really enjoys the atmosphere, it touches him. What's the effect? I'm not sure. I prefer to leave that to the One at work in Robert.

Testing the spirits

I know, of course, that man is proud by nature and that non-believers can put the good God has given them to bad use. If they do a good deed, they often take the honor for it themselves: 'See, I'm a good person, because I do good things.' I do not connect with that. If I see a person doing a good thing, I'll say I can see God at work in him. It's a way of honoring God. You ignore the empty boasting, while deliberately connecting with the good work of God. And by ignoring the pride, you avoid making a connection - through the words you speak - with latent or manifest powers of darkness. You have to stay alert! Test the spirits! If someone says, 'You see, I am a good person...,' there's something in there I can connect with: the will to be a good person. So I can respond by saying the desire to be good is God-given. 'God put that desire in your heart.' Comments like these can really help us build bridges. The opposite response would be to emphasize the spiritual gap between ourselves and that other person, for instance, by pointing at his or her unbelief. Instead, we stress the work of God in that person. That's how real connections are established: 'God is at work in me as well as in you!' If you want to tackle a person's pride about their good deeds, you could try and search for its root. Maybe there's an inferiority complex hidden beneath it. In that case, you could come alongside that person by sharing the grace of God that we all need so badly. Or by saying that God has a special love for people who are humble and contrite of heart. But you may also encounter a real, rock-hard type of pride. If you do, make sure you distance yourself from it clearly. Confrontations may occur, but watch and wait patiently to find out what is behind them. The more points of connection there are, the more receptiveness you will find for the truth of the gospel.

Exposition 1 - Types of connection: 1 Corinthians 2:12-3:9

You cannot connect with everyone in the same way

Connecting with everyone is impossible, as people can be very different spiritually.
Paul speaks of these differences in 1 Corinthians 2:12-3:9:
1. The unspiritual person. This person is led by the spirit of the world. 1 Corinthians 12:2 tells us this spirit leads people astray. It darkens their mind (Eph. 4:18).

2. **The carnal person.** The Holy Spirit has shed light in this person's mind, but this light does not penetrate his or her daily life, leaving this person unchanged. The hallmark of a carnal person is that he is incapable of connecting with the work of Jesus in people or events. He lives in jealousy and quarrelling (1 Cor. 3:3) and takes sides with human factions rather than connecting with the broader work of God (1 Cor. 3:4).
3. **The spiritual person.** This person can connect with the entire work of Jesus (1 Cor. 3:8-9, see also 2 Cor. 8:5 - the people described here first gave themselves to God and then understood this meant they must give themselves to one another also).

God created man to live in communion with others. All healthy people pursue relationships. The unspiritual person fails to see that God has given us the capacity to relate. This blindness gives rise to selfish tendencies in people. Unspiritual people think they need other people for their own development - that is the nature of the spirit of the world.

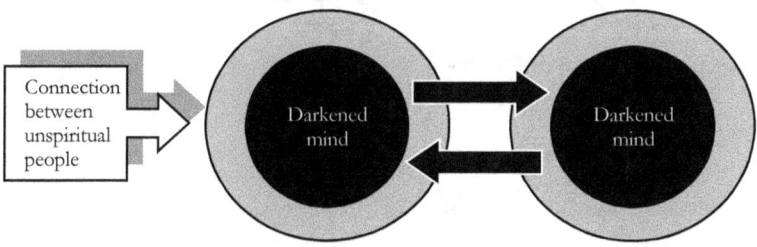

The carnal (unchanged) person knows Jesus and offers lip service to the truth, but still acts selfishly in his relationships. He looks for things/groups that will provide maximum benefit. In connecting with these events and people, he does not seek the broader work of God, neither is it his intention to serve God with his gifts.

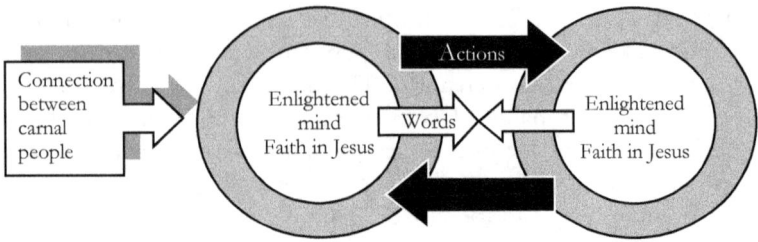

The spiritual person knows that all good things come from God and are given for our use in God's broad service (1 Cor. 3:9; 3:21-23; 10:23-24). Consequently, the spiritual person establishes relationships on that basis.

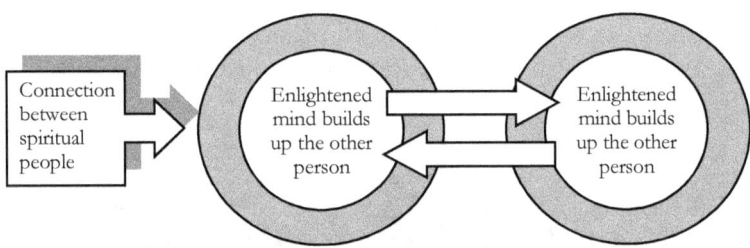

Connecting with non-believing (unspiritual) people

The spiritual person focuses on all that comes from God in creation as well as in people, in order to honor Him (1 Tim. 4:4-5; James 1:16-17). Paul did this in his encounter with the people of Athens (Acts 17:22-31) and with King Agrippa (Acts 26:26-29). Jesus wanted His disciples to pursue deeper connections with people who were open to God's peace (Matt. 10:11-13). Similarly, the spiritual person in encountering unspiritual people will seek to connect with what is from God in those people. In this way, he can be used by the Spirit to enlighten their darkened minds.

The spiritual person is used by the Spirit to recognize the work of God in other people, thus encouraging them to give themselves to God. As soon as a person surrenders to God, the Spirit begins to teach him about his spiritual family and about God's desire for him to become bound up with this family (2 Cor. 8:5).

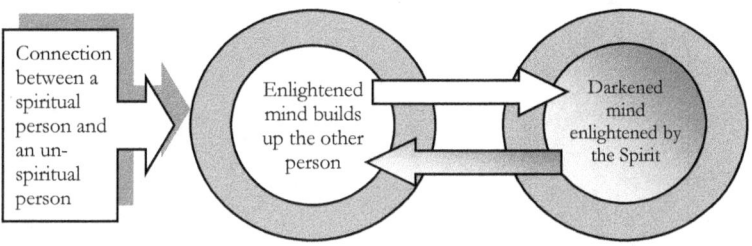

The spiritual person is trained by the Spirit to receive all that comes from God through other people. This is how the relationship grows between a spiritual parent and a spiritual child led to Christ by that parent.

End of Exposition 1 - Types of connection: 1 Corinthians 2:12-3:9

Now the big question, of course, is whether as Christians we can really step out into the world as open-mindedly as this. Whether we are entitled to pinpointing God's work in situations that are actually quite wrong. Are we allowed to connect like this with people who in some cases do not want to have anything to do with God? Is there a biblical case for this open-minded interaction with creation, even when we can see some things being used by the devil for his purposes?

7. Can a pastor freely go out into the world?

Yes, because all good things come from God

'Are you really a reverend? Then you shouldn't be in a bar, should you? Does your religion really allow you to come here and drink a beer?'

Yes, a pastor is allowed to do all of the above. But there are some mental hurdles to take on the way to becoming a regular barfly - some pretty tough ones, to be honest! You can imagine how easy it is to get a bad reputation in a small town in the Bible Belt. Churches here have some pretty strict rules as to what a reverend is supposed to do and what he is not supposed to do. Through choices I made I rudely shattered some of those rules as far as the villagers are concerned. A reverend sitting at a bar with a guy the size of a tree right behind him swinging his hips like an oversexed adolescent? And another guy as drunk as a monkey, leaning over to place a drooling kiss on the reverend's fluffy grey hair and almost hugging him to bits? These are definitely not the kind of images town folk associate with a man of the cloth!

Or picture this: a servant of the Lord being lifted off the ground and hung upside down above the ground, just for fun, by two pot-smoking boys. The victim knows the stunt is well-meant, but can't help praying he won't be dropped. Is that really the pastor? It's kind of unusual in a respectable town like ours. However, these images are all taken from real experiences I've had - and I could add many similar ones. In fact, I remember these things with great fondness. But is that acceptable? How could it be justified? What about holiness?

Learn to receive from the world

My answer to the above questions is simple: that tree-size guy and those pot smokers, in their own ways, were expressing affection for me. Which is a good thing! And whatever is good comes from God. The folks in the bars and pubs know who I am. If one of them shares something good with me, I am free to receive it from God's hand as if it were a cup of cold water (Matt. 10:42). This is the lesson James teaches us: 'Every good gift and every perfect gift is from above, and cometh down from the Father of lights' (James 1:17).

Now this can get complicated, because the power belonging to Pontius Pilate was also given him from above (John 19:11). He corrupted it, however, by allowing the Jewish leaders to blackmail him. So good and perfect gifts can be used in very wrong ways. But that doesn't make the good bad! Wrongful usage of a good thing is not the same as the good thing itself. We may sanctify what is good with thanksgiving and prayer (1 Tim. 4:4-5). It is a fact that God gives good gifts without respect of persons or things. Jesus taught us this in the Sermon on the Mount. He referred to God's generosity in order to set us an example. Just as God the Father 'maketh His sun to rise on the evil and on the good, and sendeth rain on the just and on the unjust,' so we, too, must be generous to all (Matt. 5:45). What those evil or unjust people end up doing with God's good gifts does not affect God's behavior. And regardless of people's response, what is good remains good. That's the first thing to remember.

The second thing is that all good things ultimately are intended for God's children (1 Cor. 3:21-23) to receive with thanksgiving (1 Tim. 4:4-5). Even meat sacrificed to idols may be eaten with thanksgiving (1 Cor. 10:25-30). Just as the accomplishments of the Canaanites, along with all the goodness of their culture and land, were intended for Israel (Deut. 19:1; Josh. 1:3), so it is today. Not that we will receive all good things before Jesus returns - in fact, sometimes we receive very, very little. But that does not change the fact that all good things are ultimately intended for us (Matt. 5:5; Rom. 8:19). That's why Paul could write that meat torn from the mouths of idols, as it were, can be eaten in the service of

God. Just like that. Paul did a warning, though. Believers in his day were not to partake in anything and everything. The Bible instructs us to test the spirits, to be aware of the direction in which a spirit wants to take us. Believers are told to learn to discern pride, evil powers and evil desires drifting along with certain spirits and to back away from them immediately! We are allowed to receive the good, but we are to avoid following in the direction in which idolatrous spirits seek to take disobedient people. So stay away from spirits and idols, and stay focused on what builds up the church! This means we can approach the world open-mindedly, as long as we keep discerning the spirits.

Some people may struggle to understand this. Their criticism of this attitude may stem from a lack of understanding. This is a sad thing, because lack of understanding can actually hinder the development of the church. This is an important point! If people try to keep you from going to pubs and bars and other 'dens of iniquity' to meet sinners and seekers with the purpose of winning them for Jesus, they are not keeping the growth of the church in mind. Instead, they are acting from a false kind of piety that hinders the growth of the church. Our enemy is the real source of this kind of criticism thrown at someone who visits bars in the name of Jesus. Obviously, we must try not offend people, but if our aim is to help build up the church, we're free. I go out into the world freely to claim whatever good I find there for the Kingdom of God.

This may sound like tough talking, but you can also see it as a way of acquiring the right kind of boldness. The casual atmosphere at the pub is meant for me. The beauty of the mosque is meant for me. The love I receive from a drunkard is meant for me. Believe me, I have received a lot of love on my visits to bars - and it's usually a lot more spontaneous than it is in the organized church! We do have to stay alert in dealing with 'pub love': sometimes it is about as deep and as trustworthy as a muddy creek! I don't recommend 'diving in' without restraint. Test the waters with your feet first, carefully, to see if you can feel the bottom. Then check whether it spreads to greater depth or not. You may be in for some truly beautiful experiences. Like getting to know that woman who is held in contempt by everyone, yet embraces our group as her true family. Or the love of that guy who is an alcoholic. He has become so fond of me over time that his door is always open to me - even though at times he refuses to open it for his so-called friends. I've noticed I really matter to him and he has come to really matter to me as well! The good of this world is meant for God's children.

Paul wrote that the world is ours, but that we are Christ's and Christ is God's (1 Cor. 3:22-23). This grants us an amazing openness toward the world - an openness that allows us to go out into the world freely and with boldness (Matt. 28:18-20).

It is meant for us

To make sure we understand this point properly, I'd like to outline again how things have been arranged. All the good the devil received from God is meant for us. The devil, you see, is no more than a highly gifted creature. Without all those good gifts he received or stole from God, he would collapse like an empty bag. He is an angel originally created to serve us like all the other angels (1 Cor. 6:3; Heb. 1:14). But his pride led him to believe he could do without God and he stole the gifts given to him in order to use them for his own purposes. Jesus said he came 'to steal, and to kill, and to destroy.' (John 10:10).

But the devil does a lot more. He oppresses people he is supposed to be serving with his gifts (Acts 10:38) and abuses them, like slaves, for his own glory. Like the thief and the murderer that he is, he robs people of the good things they have received from God in order to enhance his own power and glory (Matt. 4:8-9). In his pride, he has amassed quite a lot of glory for himself. But around the year 33 AD, things took a nasty turn for him. We owe that to Jesus. And now we are free to go out into the world with Him to recover for the God's Kingdom all the good things stashed away by the devil. We are to bring back what belongs to Jesus (Matt. 12:29-30). On the Day of Judgment, God will take from the devil all the good he has been misusing, and the realm of the devil will collapse (Heb. 12:26-29). Everything we see of that realm today only remains standing because God has allowed His goodness to remain in it. When God comes with His purifying fire, we will 'put on immortality' in order to pass through that fire (1 Cor. 15:50-53). Then the city of God's goodness will descend in all its fullness, and 'the glory and honor of the nations' will be brought into it (Rev. 21:26).

Whenever I enter a bar or a mosque, I go there to receive what is of God here and now. Hopefully, I go there under the guidance of the Spirit to retrieve from those places what belongs in God's Kingdom. The first way of doing this is to thank God for all the good I receive in those places. I consciously honor Him for the beauty I encounter. In doing so, I give the devil's pride a knock and lift up God - even in places where the devil thought he had all the power. My approach is simple: honor God everywhere, for God inhabits praise (Ps. 22:3). The devil does not like that, and I like taking away his pleasure. That's how we can go out into the world.

Now let's take a look at how Jesus did it. Why did Jesus come into this world and face poverty so severe that He did not even have a place to lay His head (Matt. 8:20)? Because He boldly expected God to place people on His path who would serve Him with their gifts (Luke 8:3). Why did He send out His disciples without provisions? So that they would learn to receive from the world (Matt. 10:10; 1 Cor. 9:11). Whoever goes out into the world with empty hands is demonstrating that he has not just come to pass on God's love, but also to receive tokens of love from the world. Whoever goes out into the world with an attitude that suggests the world needs *him*, because *he*, being a servant of God, has it all, will come across as proud and offensive. That is the feeling that is often expressed by people who run into one of those puffed-up 'evangelists.' Evangelists like that fail to connect with what is small and humble and thereby remain inaccessible to seeking people. They are not like Jesus! Jesus was 'meek and lowly in heart' (Matt. 11:29) and in coming into the world like that, He demonstrated a willingness to receive from the world whatever God wanted to give Him in the world (John 6:39). His disciples went out in the same faith.

A new command of sanctification

Some Christians do not think we can go out into the world as freely as this. They're mistaken. It's a mistake that is easy to understand: they are basing their viewpoint on an old sanctification command. According to this old command, God's people were to separate themselves from the Gentiles (Lev. 20:26). Christians living by that old command like to maintain an alternative culture. They do all they can to emphasize that they are different. They like to keep a broad moat between the evil outside world and their island of piety. The whole idea of connecting with Greeks by becoming like a Greek and with Jews by becoming like a Jew, with athletes by becoming like an athlete and with bar crawlers by visiting bars is lost on them (1 Cor. 9:19-23).

Maybe they're afraid that connecting with other people means you will somehow immediately adopt those people's sinful behavior. What a foolish notion (John 17:15-17)! It starts with misunderstanding the fact that since the Great Commission, God has introduced a new way of living a holy life. We can only achieve holiness by doing what God commands. And if He commands us to go out into the world, the only way to live a holy life is to obey your calling and go out into the world (1 Pet. 1:14-17; 2:9-10)!

As we recognize that all the good in the world comes only from God and is meant for His children, as an inheritance, we begin to understand that we are free to enjoy things like sports and culture. That doesn't mean things cannot get complicated at times. I remember a really exciting tennis match being played between a Dutch player and some foreign champion. It was broadcast on TV. Now the sports performance was really amazing to watch. It was a good thing meant for me and all God's children to enjoy. But behind the event, there was a sickening commercialism aimed expressly at manipulating people. The sponsor was intent on gaining a monopoly in a certain section of the market. That is a satanic attitude. So there were a lot of things going on that were being used to honor the devil. But one thing made me switch off the TV at a certain point. It was when the Dutch player started cursing terribly about his mistakes. That was something I could simply not connect with. His constant swearing annoyed me ... I hated it! This is an example of something good given by God, but ruined by the devil. As children of God, we must decide at which point our enjoyment of God's good gifts becomes impossible.

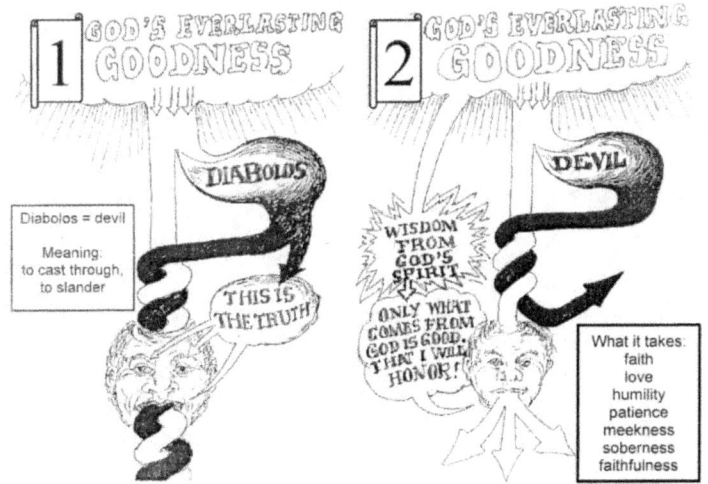

In the first picture, you can see the devil misusing God's good gifts for the dark purposes of his realm. A person who does not have the Spirit can be blinded to the goodness of God and may begin to see reality as a chaotic mess.

In the second picture, you can see a person who has God's Spirit exposing the work of the devil. This person has opened himself up to the fruit of the Spirit and he recognizes the beautiful work of God, regardless of the devil's deceptions, and can connect with that good work.

Can we freely go out into the world, just like that?

How do we recognize when things have gone wrong?

Is there a way of knowing something has entered into our hearts that does not belong there?

How do we preserve our spiritual freedom?

These are the questions I'd like to consider in the next chapter.

8. How do you keep yourself free and bold?

A brief study of Cain, who lost his freedom

As soon as we ask ourselves what lessons we have to learn in order to go out into the world boldly, our attention is drawn to that attitude of boldness. How do you develop it? How do you act freely, and confidently, in the face of the powers of this world? Remember, we can only go out into the world if we hold on to this confidence. The word confidence occurs in Hebrews 10:35, among other places. This passage instructs us never to let go of our confidence. It will help us in a world of temptations, lies and trials. Hebrews 11 gives us a long list of things we may face in this complicated world of ours. By faith, you can remain standing. The Greek word for confidence is *parrèsia*. It suggests freedom to act. Where does this freedom come from? It is a freedom that has become reality through what transpired - and is still transpiring - in heaven. In heaven, the blood of Jesus was sacrificed, and on account of that sacrifice Jesus pleads our case, our freedom. Since this freedom has been secured for us by Jesus, we have 'boldness to enter into the holiest' (Hebr. 10:19). In other words, this freedom, or confidence, exists only within an open connection between you and heaven - through the blood of Jesus. The devil's aim is to break, or disturb, the connection, by drawing your attention away from it.

Take a look at the beginning of the Bible. You'll find two key stories there about people who lost their freedom. Now the question is: what do these stories teach us about the process of losing our freedom? Do they reveal telltale signs of steps you might be taking towards losing your freedom, your confidence? The answer is: yes, they do! You might say sin is the predator of freedom, because the fact is... it is through sin that freedom is lost. Does that mean no one has grounds for confidence, since 'all have sinned' (Rom. 3:23), and 'there is none righteous' (Rom. 3:10-11)? Our confidence does not depend on our sinless conduct - if there ever is such a thing - but on the blood of Jesus. It's like standing at a fork in the road. In one direction, you see your struggle against sin and in the other direction you see the blood of Jesus. That blood, in essence, is the pure love of God! Now, at a fork in the road, you can only go in one direction at once. The question is: to which side are you going to direct your attention? Toward your behavior and achievements, or toward God's love? Are you living in your own strength or in God's love? Your freedom can indeed be lost as a result of sin. But remember: sin's attacks always begin with the temptation to live in your own strength! Sin wants to draw you into a way of living that centers on you! At all costs, it wants to direct your attention away from God's love for you.

The first story

The first story from Genesis we're going to look at shows how this works. After eating the forbidden fruit, Adam and Eve were caught in the stranglehold of self-centeredness. They were ashamed. The serpent had opened their eyes to their actual position. Immediately, they began to judge themselves. Paul knew how dangerous this is: judging oneself (1 Cor. 4:3-5). The first humans began to be occupied with themselves.[6] To live in their own strength. They wanted more... surely, they were entitled to more! They wanted to be god-like. A god is a judge (Ex. 21:6). He decides where to draw the line. A person who desires to be god-like wants to determine where the boundaries lie between good and evil. Adam and Eve felt this authority should be theirs. They became prisoners of their desire to judge! This focus on self-judgment and self-determination comes from the devil. He, too, decided to live for himself. He wanted to be god-like. He

---

[6] The cause was the *deception* of Eve by the serpent. The bait was 'becoming like God,' and God is *good*, so what could be wrong about that? Well, you can't *become* like God by *disobeying* Him.

felt it was his right. His future became a hell. Adam and Eve wanted the same thing. Their efforts ended in failure. They had to hide away and cover themselves with aprons made from fig leaves. Any person wishing to hide away cannot possibly be free!

The second story

The second sin mentioned in the Bible also results in loss of freedom. When Cain was angry with Abel, he lost the ability to go out into the world freely and withdrew within himself. A loss of freedom is always a sign of the presence of sin. It may not express itself in external acts, but there is a sense of un-freedom. In the palace of Caiaphas, Peter denied he was a friend of Jesus. His fear robbed him of his freedom and he started to lie.

David lost his freedom after getting Bathsheba pregnant. He started acting as if he was a friend of her husband, Uriah. But Uriah did not know this friendship was merely a mask. Behind the mask, David was hatching wicked plans. Both Peter and David knew in their hearts that they were not free. This sense of not being free is always a warning signal: as soon as you are aware of it, you should know something is wrong. If a man is talking with a woman in a bar and his eyes are constantly attracted to her low neckline, then he is not free. A woman may be beautiful and there's nothing wrong with noticing it, or even thanking God for it! Good looks are good looks! But as soon as you sense you are losing your ability to thank God for what you see and you'd prefer Him not to know what you are thinking about this woman - in other words, as soon as you cease to look at this person from the point of view of God's love - you have become captive to self-centeredness. You begin to live for yourself. You lose your freedom. You begin to lose your confidence. If this goes on for too long, you will have more and more trouble giving thanks. You will become a prisoner of your own hypocrisy.

And your behavior will demand more and more of your attention. You will be pretending to be pious, but it will be unreal and un-free. A true prayer of thanksgiving is completely free! Lack of freedom is a sign of misdirected attention. If you keep having to talk about yourself, you can be sure there is something wrong. You are not free. If you cannot do without success, you know there's something wrong. If as a pastoral counselor you develop contacts that take away your freedom, or hinder you from looking at the world freely and confidently, something has happened that is not good. 'Where the Spirit of the Lord is, there is liberty' (2 Cor. 3:17). Sometimes you have to do things for the sake of another person's weakness. If you do this out of pure love for that person, you'll find that it will not affect your freedom. You can act for the sake of that other person, even if he or she is imprisoned by fixed habits or a blind following of rules: you can go along with the rules, because you know there are important issues at stake. But if your motive is not love, you will sense a loss of freedom.

In the previous chapter, we asked what it takes to go out into the world confidently. The answer is that we must guard our hearts, knowing that what enters in will begin to take control over our behavior (Prov. 4:23). This does not just apply to people engaged in street work, but to all God's children. We must all be on the alert for the warning signals of diminishing freedom. It always starts with a loss of freedom in how you direct your attention.

There's something confusing about sin. It gives you the impression you are deliberately choosing something, because it appeals to you. You want that kick! You want that little adventure! Or, more dangerously, you want that deceitful peace and quiet of pretending you don't have a calling. You choose to bury your talent under the ground. You may use fine words, such as 'I have to keep myself from this sinful world and from temptation,' and it may sound like this is your own choice. In actual fact, however, you have allowed fear and insecurity to take control. You are no longer being guided by God's love. You are afraid of failing in the world or of missing out on experiences. You are allowing your own desires to rule your life. You've lost your freedom. You're losing your vision of God's love for you. You're standing at the fork in the road and looking in the wrong direction. Jesus instructed us to face the trials ahead of us without fear, because He 'has overcome the world' (John 16:33). Do not fool yourself. Do not underestimate the enemy. Sin is so smart, it can kid you into believing you're free, when you're not (2 Pet. 2:19). Sin has chosen you. It has seen you looking in the wrong direction and crept up on you. Paul wrote that he did things he didn't want to do (Rom. 7:20). The Bible says this always happens gradually. Cain sensed that sin was lying at the door of his life, poised to strike (Gen. 4:7). He was told to rule over sin, to say to sin, 'Go away from my door. I don't want to let you in. I don't want you near me. I don't even want to give you my attention! I want to be able to move about freely. I choose to direct my attention towards God's love for me.'

So what can we learn from the attack on Cain's life? How did things unfold for him? Had he become weakened by something at some earlier stage? It's possible. Perhaps being the firstborn male he had been put on a pedestal. It's not hard to imagine. After the fall, Eve's freedom had been severely weakened. But she had been told that the way to freedom would be reopened through childbirth. Then came their first child. After the difficulties of pregnancy and the pain of delivery, there he was: a boy! 'I have gotten a man from the Lord!' You can almost feel danger closing in. This little boy could easily become the center of attention in a very unhealthy way. As he grew up, Cain naturally felt he must be pretty important. And when he brought a sacrifice to God, it was little more than a ritual to him. It was just one of those things you did. Ultimately, Cain himself, being Eve's firstborn son, was more important than God. So Cain pursued a life devoted to himself. Abel also brought a sacrifice. He did it wholeheartedly. He did not live for himself, but in connection, especially with God. He stood at the fork in the road and looked in the right direction.

The first step

This is the first step towards giving in to the sin that lies at our door:

1. Living for yourself without connecting with others.

People who live for themselves have a serious lack of love. People who seek to connect with others and are prepared to bind up the wounds of others must, of necessity, learn to love. There's nothing strange about crying your heart out about someone else's need. Perhaps we should say that you cannot be a pastoral counselor if you do not cry for others from time to time. Confidence and boldness are nothing like stoicism; they are about connecting with the lordship of Jesus. And His rule is one of loving kindness. One of labor pains. A friend of mine who came to Christ once said, 'Compassion is a beautiful form of pain.' That's what love does. Love feels like this delicious freedom, but is bound up with things you would strongly dislike if you did not have love. If you don't have love, you'll hate having to listen to people complaining and whining. But if you love, you gravitate towards people; you look for the real person behind the words, or the complaints. You push through the 'whining' and get to the heart of the matter. A person who does not have love will hate the very thought of having to do things for other people.

Think about this: love does things only love can do - love connects duty to pleasure. Love senses exactly what needs to be done, or avoided, and acts accordingly. And the end result is joy! A person who lovingly obeys the commands of Jesus, will always be filled with joy (John 15:11). People who have love do not love for and in themselves, but in connection. Cain couldn't do that. But he saw that Abel could. He noticed that God was connected with Abel, and Cain sensed he was missing out in this most vital part of life. As he entertained this feeling, sin crept a little closer. At this point, Cain should have fallen to his knees. He should have sought to reconnect with God through prayer. But he didn't. Instead, he let sin creep a little closer still.

The second step

2. Self-pity creeps in.

Self-pity causes us to become even more occupied with ourselves. You sense you're missing out on something and you feel sorry for yourself for not having what that other person has. You feel deprived... a victim! You feel you deserve some comforting. You need an embrace - not with the purpose of entering into a relationship, not because you are seeking to connect with that other person, but because you feel you're important, or have been short-changed. People engaging in street work or pastoral counseling should never do it for the sake of gaining recognition or appreciation. Approaching people with that in mind is the same as opening the door to sin. Your focus is on what you're missing out on, while you fail to see what you are really lacking - a connection with God and people around you. You are living in and for yourself. Your 'poor little me' wants to be comforted. You want your poor little me to be embraced or appreciated. But you'll soon find out that this will not get you what you really need. It will not lead to real connection. You will still be self-imprisoned.

In Genesis, we read that Cain's 'countenance fell.' The empty feeling he had was no longer some vague misgiving, but a feeling caused by his brother. Those dark feelings inside him began to find a focal point: 'It's all because of him!' Cain's sense of emptiness was now so intense that sin was able to make its next move. There was still a way out for Cain, but the enemy's power over him had now grown so strong that turning around was more difficult than ever.

The third step

3. Envy makes the heart sick.

Jealousy, or envy, is an inner attitude of comparing your situation with someone else's and seeing that this other person has something you feel should be yours. In allowing this attitude to gain a place in your mind, you are judging both yourself and that other person. But only God can judge, as only He is all-knowing. Entertaining jealousy, then, means taking God's place! It is what the devil wants - and what was to be the beginning of his downfall. Jesus says we must neither judge nor condemn (Luke 6:37). He also says in Luke that we must let go - a poignant instruction in this context! We want to take things into our own hands. Judging someone gives us the feeling we have a measure of control over that person. We've assigned him or her a place: this is what he or she is like. It is a way of distancing ourselves from that person. Jesus tells us to let go, so that we will be let go. You may pretend you are connected with that person, by exerting control over him, but in reality you are trying to hold him in an unhealthy grip. Not because you want to be connected, but because you want to be superior. You are placing yourself above the other person. You are creating distance between yourself and him, or her. You do not see that person as someone worth embracing, but as some moving object you need to control. This happens so often in pastoral work, and even more so in evangelism! Just listen to the prayers that are said before and after the activity. It's as if the people praying know exactly what spiritual bonds there are and who is heading to hell, as if they have charted the other person's life right down to the last detail. You're the evangelist, you know these things! Meanwhile, your pastoral attitude is soured by preconceived ideas. Jesus tells us we must not judge like that. Note the immediate context: this commandment is placed in between two others. Right before this, Jesus instructs us to 'be merciful' (Luke 6:36); right after it, He says we must 'give' (Luke 6:38). Mercy and giving are acts by which you connect with others. That's what Jesus is talking about. He wants us to look for what God has given us in that other person and connect with him or her on that basis. So there you are, at the fork in the road, and you can look at the other person as an object for you to take advantage of, or you can look at him or her from the perspective of God's love. Do the latter, and you will recognize what God is doing in his or her life. And what God is giving you. It is an attitude of praising God in your relationships with others. Passing judgment is off limits, as it means placing yourself above the other person by sizing him up, by saying something final about him. So if we're not to judge, what are we supposed to do when we go out into the world? We are to 'try the spirits' (1 John 4:1).

What's the difference? When we judge people, we pass a final sentence on them. 'That guy is an incurable drunkard.' 'That woman has always been a whore.' 'He is a hypocritical churchgoer.' 'She'll never let you down.' 'Only with her will I ever be happy.' 'I will always help everyone.' These are all statements that far exceed our understanding. They fix our thinking in unchangeable opinions that are usually far from the truth. Besides, everything you might say about a person today may be different tomorrow. God can change people.

There's another thing. Fixed judgments cause us to lose our freedom. Judgments and preconceived ideas will corrode our confidence, turning people and things into unchangeable forces! In our minds, they become stronger than God. The result is that all kinds of fears and misplaced certainties enter in. Such as: bars are always evil, and churches are always good. But if you hear someone mentioning the name of Jesus or God with reverence, it is always good. We have to learn to look at the undercurrent of pious words spoken, seeing through insincere manipulation. If you're judgmental, you'll automatically consider someone who curses to be doing evil. You're not learning to identify the seeking spirit behind the cursing. Trying, or testing, the spirits means you sense the undercurrent in a person's life. His or her actions may be wrong, but you do not judge the person, as that is God's prerogative. So always be aware of the spiritual movement going on. It's important to us. Spirits can be felt just as the wind (John 3:8). They exert pressure in a certain direction. Do you sense someone's spirit moving towards - or away from - the character of Christ and the grace of God? As we learn to sense the movement of the spirits, we become aware of the fact that things can always take surprising turns. In these movements we see the freedom of God's creativity. Situations can suddenly change. You can look freely at what God is doing. This is all part of the confidence we may enjoy.

If you are not experienced in trying the spirits, you're likely to make big mistakes in pastoral work as well as in street work. You'll fall into the devil's trap, keeping people at a distance by judging them. That's what the devil always does: accuse people (Rev. 12:10). Cain began to look for a scapegoat to cover up his own shortcoming. He could have easily solved his problem by giving himself to God heart and soul. Instead, he withdrew further into self-pity and jealousy. He began to accuse Abel, allowing sin to come closer. Cain assumed the role of a judge. In his heart he condemned Abel.

The fourth step

4. You are filled with anger.

Cain received a warning as his heart filled with anger: Why are you withdrawing? If nothing is bothering you, you can look at the world confidently and freely, can't you? 'Why art thou wroth? And why is thy countenance fallen?' (Gen. 4:6) The warning was worded in such a way that Cain would have been able to recognize his own behavior. But people who are caught up in their own pain do not easily heed a warning. This last attempt to fix things was lost on Cain. He was already planning to kill his brother. In his mind, he was already out in the field, where he would be free to strike. How scary it is to think we can be so filled with loathing that we no longer see our brother or neighbor as he really is. And that we can block out God's warnings. That people can head straight for disaster in total blindness...

Why did God not intervene? Why didn't He stop Cain? Questions like these can be tough for those engaged in pastoral work. If you find yourself asking too many questions like this one, you need to stop quickly. You're looking for answers that are beyond your understanding. Job did the same thing. He decided God was unfair. He lost his confidence before God and started getting impertinent. As if Job knew more than God.

Part of holding onto your confidence is not allowing yourself to get stuck on tough issues - even when everything seems to be falling apart. Even if you have literally ended up in prison, you can still be free. Even in a situation that appears to be a total deadlock, a confident person can let go. Let go and retain your freedom. God Himself remained free in the situation with Cain. He did not force Cain into anything, nor did He let Cain force him. Instead, He was guided by His love. We do not have to understand the ways of God, but we may rest in His wisdom - even when everything seems to have gone wrong.

What about Abel? Did God let go of Abel? No! God said to Cain, 'The voice of thy brother's blood crieth unto me from the ground' (Gen. 4:10) and Abel's blood still speaks today (Heb. 12:24). God remains connected to Abel. This means that one day, in His own divine way, He will right the wrong done to Abel! Only He can do it and He wants us to leave the matter in His hands. Cain failed to understand this. He was blinded to it, because his heart had been poisoned by anger. Cain decided to take things into his own hands.

The fifth step

5. Murder.

Cain's resentment of his brother's happiness caused him to resent his brother - to the point that he decided he had to get rid of him. You can get rid of someone in a lot of different ways. You can make life so difficult for him that he gets sick. Sometimes people are so painfully aware of the fact that they have been rejected that they end up killing, or injuring, themselves. People need God's love. What we have just considered teaches us that living of oneself means getting rid of others (and injuring ourselves). In Cain's life, it's easy to see sin closing on him.

1. It all began when he started to consider himself the center of everything. He broke the connection.
2. Then self-pity entered in. He didn't get what he wanted and felt he was being victimized.
3. Then Cain started looking for someone to blame. He became an accuser.
4. His next step was to set himself up as judge. He passed sentence on his brother.
5. Finally, Cain became the executor of the sentence he had passed.

Sin's attack on Cain is very instructive. What's so revealing about it is that sin creeps into our heart little by little. If we are on our guard, we will notice. At each step, we will find ourselves losing more of our freedom. You start to live for yourself and the world becomes something you merely feed on in many different ways.

Because of your self-centeredness, this food will never satisfy you. You're standing at the fork in the road, looking the wrong way. A person living for himself cannot receive God's love from the world. But a person seeking God's love in the world will be amazed at how much he finds out there. He can go out freely and discover God's abundance. This freedom is his position in Christ. In Christ, he holds a very special position. In Him, he has been liberated before God to enjoy God's victory freely and joyfully. And he is free to establish relationships in the world the way God wants him to. He'll make a great pastoral worker!

Street work centers on developing new relationships all the time and on looking for ways to expand on them, creating communities that will flourish in the light of God's love. A complete relationship always consists of three things. You have to know how to communicate love at three levels:

1. An intellectual level.
2. An emotional level.
3. A physical level.

Evangelism often takes place strictly on the intellectual level. You explain the basic tenets of the Gospel and if your listener accepts them, you've saved a soul. The listener more or less has to admit the evangelist is right; his view is the right one. The convert recognizes this and wants to accept the truth. This can be the beginning of a relationship, but I think Jesus teaches us to develop relationships that are full and complete from the start. The question is how. We'll look at that in the next chapter. In dealing with this question, I'd like to start by looking at what people usually notice first about us: our physical presence.

9. How do you communicate love?

Your physical presence is the first thing people notice about you

'I'm not a believer at all. I believe in science, evolution. But I still feel like talking to you, because you're always sitting here and you look so friendly.' Sitting down on the bar stool next to mine, that is how Marjory introduced herself to me. Her bright eyes looked at me curiously. Her open approach really took me by surprise. I liked it! And that's how it goes. The first thing we communicate is usually our facial expression. If you're at peace inwardly, it will show in your body. If you're tense, or happy, those around you will feel it. Our body is important in making contact with other people.

I love showing affection, so it's easy for me to give someone a hug. To me, this is one of the main ingredients of 'evangelism.' It's my way of showing someone I want to connect with him. In our youth center, I often notice how the 'cool guys' use their bodies to show they are connected. They can say really hurtful things. Really bad stuff. You'd think they must have terrible fights. But it's not true: even their verbal abuse is subject to clear codes; they belong together and often they express this with body language.

Basically, we have three groups of young people at Building 33. The way they greet each other reflects which group they belong to. The members of one group will clasp hands or give each other a box, or fist bump. I always feel honored when one of these guys comes over to me and says, 'Pastor... box!' It involves knocking your fists together in a certain way and is sometimes followed by a pretty complicated hand ritual that ends with giving each other a tap on the chest. Among the bars and pubs I visit, the Korevaar[7] pub is probably my home base. On arriving or leaving, I always have some form

---

[7] Pronounce 'Kore' as 'core' and 'vaar' as 'var' in 'varsity.'

of physical contact, giving almost everyone there a light touch - except for newcomers or folks I've never talked to before.

There are definite rules about that, too. Some guys will come over and hug me. I learned I have to restrain my enthusiasm when it turned out once I had bruised some ribs - once I even broke a guy's rib! Geniality has no bounds. Occasionally, I meet guys who can't handle it. In some cases, I have found out later they were physically or sexually abused in childhood.

Using body language in relationships with women is a lot more complicated. As long as there are other folks around, such as in a pub, there's not much that can go wrong. But you always have to be alert. Some women deliberately go after men. In some cases, their dads may not have shown them enough physical tenderness when they were younger. A bar is a great place to catch up on that! A few drinks may cause such a woman to really get close to a man, as alcohol tends to blur the boundaries of physical contact. Thankfully, the fact that I am a reverend naturally discourages this kind of behavior and I'm glad about that. But if you visit bars and pubs to do street work you have to be very alert in this area, or you may wind up a prisoner and lose your freedom. Always be aware of the person you are dealing with. Which spirit is at work in him or her? How can you make sure the relationship remains pure? In contacts with women, this is a very dangerous field.

Every study ever done on touch shows that human beings cannot live without physical contact. As a fetus in your mother's womb, you began to experience life in the embrace of the amniotic fluid. Our sense of touch is the first sense to tell us we're alive.

The simple fact that touch is so vital to our existence means the devil will do all he can to ruin things in this area. There are two ways in which he does this. Either he tempts us to ignore appropriate boundaries or he tries to impose all kinds of unhealthy strictures on us. In the latter case, our experience of touch becomes so cramped that we start disliking and eventually avoiding it.

The moment you sense there is the slightest sexual hint in your physical contact with someone, you need to back out quickly. Be completely clear about where you stand and prayerfully consider whether you should continue the contact and, if so, how.

We should adopt the same attitude in any situation involving alcohol. If someone has been drinking, you can never be sure what will be left of your contact after the intoxication has subsided. The sense of connection you experienced while the other person was under the influence of alcohol may have completely evaporated the next day. In some situations, a person wanting to share something painful or embarrassing with you may not have the courage to speak openly about it, without having had a few drinks first. The question is how to handle this wisely. The fact is that people tend to talk - and use body language - a lot more freely in a bar or a pub! Sometimes, loud music will reduce your conversation to a lip reading exercise. In those situations body language is also important.

Body language training

I believe we need far more training in this field. God's children should learn how to handle their bodies properly. Pure touch represents a fundamental language for reaching people at a deeper level. Pastors should learn how to read body language and how to use it. Theological training centers should incorporate it in their programs. I mean, very practically! What happens when you touch someone? What is safe and what isn't? Which alternatives can you choose from? I always look for different forms. In order to show a woman I really want to connect without actually embracing her, I might tap a fist against her upper arm. But even that slight touch may in some cases be too much. I always have to ask myself in these situations how I am keeping a watch on my own heart. This is something I can't do on my own. So I always make a point of discussing with my wife everything I feel uneasy about, whether it is my own behavior or the other person's behavior (if you're not married, you should share these things with a close friend). This firm resolve has become the watch dog in my emotional life. Whenever I am counseling a woman and it starts getting intense, I insist on involving another woman, even if it's just to safely mop up the tears! Honesty is a great guardian of your freedom! Fortunately, I have been blessed with a very wise wife who always has good advice and has protected me from a lot of mistakes. Training and openness are vital in this whole area.

The danger of living in a cramp

I mentioned living in a cramp as one of the methods the devil uses. You often see it. Counselors are often warned about the sexual tension that may emerge in a pastoral relationship, but rarely about getting into a cramp about it. I understand how cramped attitudes develop. Yet I believe they need to be dealt with. It starts with complete honesty toward ourselves and others. Unfortunately, this honesty is often hard to find. What essentially is a vital channel of love becomes clogged by 'thou-shalt-nots': thou shalt neither touch nor speak openly about the subject of touch. This approach is a recipe for sexual indiscretions. Suppressed feelings may eventually burst out in unrestrained sexual behavior, for instance, in the form of a secret addiction to pornography.

Touch within a spiritual family

As Christians, we say we are a spiritual family. If we're serious about this idea, it has implications! A family that fails to incorporate healthy physical contact among its members will end up with psychologically sick family members. The absence of touch causes illness. Healthy physical contact boosts intimacy. Having fellowship with God and one another is impossible without intimacy. Physical contact beyond your own personal boundaries or those of the other person will destroy intimacy, causing terrible damage. But Jesus embraced children, kissed his friends and allowed a woman to touch his feet as expressions of sanctified intimacy. In doing these things, Jesus set an example for Christian fellowship - and also for street work. People want authenticity - not just in the words they hear us speak, but in the whole of our conduct. That's how we can prove whether we are trustworthy or not. Being trustworthy in this most vulnerable of areas is of great value.

In my first congregation, there was an elderly lady who just could not imagine the meaning of these lines in a Dutch hymn based on Psalm 103:5: 'Just as a father lovingly embraces his child, so God our Father embraces us, for we belong to Him.' The words meant nothing to her. It turned out that when she was a child, her father had never ever touched or hugged her. Whenever I visited her, together with Carolien, I made sure I gave her a gentle hug before I left. Six months later, her image of God changed. She was getting to know Him as a Father and beginning to long for Him the way a child longs to be with his father.

Our facial expression or body language is often the first thing other people notice about us. We should speak the language of love with our whole being, including the physical. But how do you actually live this kind of love? What will our focus be if we are driven by real love? And how can we persevere in loving people like that?

10. What is real love?

Let everything about you be a channel of God's love

There is such a need for real love! With real love I mean God's love. The word love itself does not carry a lot of meaning. Some people love boxing. Others love visiting a prostitute once in a while. Spiders love flies. They'll do anything to catch one, preparing for the hunt by weaving a web, rushing on the fly once it is stuck in the web. Then they will carefully wrap it up and suck out its insides. They really love those tasty little flies.

Love focuses on something and can exert immense power in trying to get what it wants. The key question is what it is focused on. Is our love really focused on other people just as they are in God's eyes - not as people who are of interest to us for this or that reason, but as individuals in whom God is at work? We only can be if we ourselves are filled with God's love for us, I mean, for each of us as a separate person! It all centers on that strange and wonderful entity we call a 'person.' But what is a person? It's a mystery we need to try and look into. And in order to do this, we must first understand the difference between a person and an individual.

Person or individual?

The word person (in Latin: *persona*) originated in the world of classical drama. In drama, people enact a play together. The ways in which they are related to each other in the drama make them into who they are. You become a 'persona' through all your various connections with other 'personae.' The more real those persons are, they more possibilities you have to become a real person. Someone who is surrounded by individuals has very little chance of becoming a person;

pure individuals cannot 'divide' themselves in order to share their lives with others.

The word individual (Latin: *in-dividus*) refers to something that cannot be divided, or shared. It exists in and of itself. A person living completely individually is perverting his character and will start resembling a moving object. If (for example) materialism rules, people begin to lose their possibilities of living as a person. They become more and more individualistic. You notice it in the way they talk about their lives. They do things and pursue things. Without realizing it, they are gradually turning themselves into living do-things, permanently occupied with their own daily habits. Real encounters with other people become less and less frequent. Conversations center on things they have done or are doing, or on looks - that is, the designs other people have created for them; their goal, after all, is to come across positively as a visible thing. But real fellowship becomes increasingly difficult (compare Dan. 2:43).

The Bible speaks about people committing themselves to lifeless objects. They attribute a certain value to those objects, but the value is never actually proven. These objects are, in fact, idols. And the Bible says those who serve them will become like them: lifeless objects with no relations (Ps. 115:8).

We are meant to become persons: each human being carries within himself the possibility to become a unique person. Thus we see a reflection of the infinite creativity of the One who is a PERSON at the very highest level: the LORD, the covenant God: Yahweh. The One who said: I AM! There is no other Name that expresses personality quite like that Name does. Neither is there any other person who can transform human beings into real persons like He can. Fellowship with this thoroughly pure Person transforms us into persons in all kinds of variations. That's what makes people so fascinating: seeing a reflection of God's endless creativity in each one.

So whoever receives God's love becomes a person. And God's love reaches out to everyone. God's aim is for His personal love to flow through us to all those other people. Let me put that in stronger terms: God wants His Personality to flow through us to others, so that people - or persons - everywhere will blossom. It's up to us to discover all those different persons by connecting with them. God's love is the source of it all. His love never aims at emptying us of ourselves. On the contrary! From Him comes everything that can make us into a real person.

The implications of all of this are far-reaching. Everything we give to God comes from His hand (1 Chron. 29:16). It's not a matter of us offering to Him, but of inner compassion from one person to another (Matt. 9:13, see also Ps. 50:9-15, 23 and Mic. 6:7-8).

God longs to receive personal gifts (2 Cor. 9:7). God wants our hearts! He wants to connect with us from one Person to another. Two things are vital, and vitally connected:

1. God is Life.
2. God is a Person.

Real life comes from the Person who is God. We were made in God's image and after His likeness (Gen. 1:26). Wherever His image disappears, creation becomes an object that can be emptied out, much like a fly being sucked empty by a spider.

All of creation knows there will be a restoration of all that is personal - creation longs deeply for people who carry this personal image (Rom. 8:19). For in that image, creatures transcend the state of being an object and are re-transformed into a personal creation of our resplendent Creator.

A person comes into being in an open connection with others. An individual cannot truly share his life with others and will only use others for his own good.

Only in contact with Him will His image remain intact in our lives. This image determines who we are in relation to Him. That's why He came into this world as a man to embrace persons and to teach us that same embrace. It is terrible that God is sometimes depicted as some anonymous, impersonal power. Why? Because the view we have of God influences and shapes us. We become like the god we worship (Ps. 115:8). If you view God as an anonymous force, you become anonymous yourself: a religious doer of things. You'll be anonymous in the sense of being depersonalized. Your name will disappear from the book of life (Rev. 21:27). How do you get your name written in the book of life? Not by participating in great things, but through God's personal love! That love, manifested in redemption, is what gets your name written in the place in which real Life exists (Luke 10:20).

I remember once having a conversation with a lady who said she did not believe the devil was an actual person. Essentially, I would say she is right. It could be argued that the devil, in essence, is a totally depersonalized being. He has lost the ability to connect with personal beings from heart to heart, person to person. He turns people into objects and thus is degraded into a living object himself. He 'loves' us the way a spider loves its prey: he wants to suck the life out of us. Like a spider eying its prey, all he sees in us is what he can get out of us.

Sadly, this is how a lot of people view other people. All they care about in their dealings with other people is what those people might do for them, how they can draw life from them. Sooner or later, they end up disappointed. Embitterment sets in and these people abandon each other. Basically, this is what Daniel was talking about when he explained Nebuchadnezzar's dream to him (Dan. 2:43). People who hurl that familiar accusation at God - 'If God were a God of love, He would never allow all this suffering in the world!' - are really displaying a complete lack of understanding of the concept of personal love. They are looking at what God can *do* for *them*. If He does a good job, He can stick around. If He doesn't give them what they want, they reject Him. They don't seek God as a Person, but as a producer of good things. This secret of personhood is God's richest and most beautiful gift to us. Personality and Life are inseparable.

As psychologists could tell you, being deprived of personal attention may cause depression and even lead to suicide. To put that more strongly: individualization and death go hand in hand. Conversely, personal love shared from one person to another goes hand in hand with true Life. That's why it's so important for us to get to know God as a Person, and that as persons we learn to connect with what is personal in other people. This is a vital truth for all forms of pastoral work, especially street work.

Making other people more beautiful

True love wants to make that other person more beautiful. Jesus shows us this pure love in its ultimate form. He was disfigured and made repulsive in order to present us holy and blameless before God's throne. In the Sermon on the Mount, Jesus explained in vivid terms what He meant. He called His disciples the salt of the earth, the light of the world, a city on a hill, and a candle on a candlestick (Matt. 5:13-16). Jesus used four different metaphors. The number four represents the four corners of the earth: it was a way of saying that this message was to pervade the entire world. Followers of Jesus are salt, light, a city and a candle, or lamp.

The remarkable thing about these images is that each one derives its value from being useful to people. Nobody takes a mouthful of salt just for the fun of it. We use salt to flavor our food. A similar thing could be said about light: nobody would enjoy staring at the brightness of the sun or at a glaring lamp for an hour. Light is not self-serving and neither is it meant to be worshiped. It is indispensable to us throughout the day; the sun serves us by shining down on us and highlighting the beauty of God's creation. You could add that light serves to show us what needs improving. Nobody takes an ugly thing and puts it on exhibit. Except the devil. He wants to embarrass us. He wants us to try and hide ourselves, or our secrets, away in shame, so that we spend our lives alone with our secrets, rather than taking them to God. One purpose of light, then, is to expose what is ugly so that it can be made beautiful. When the ugly disappears, the beautiful gains more beauty (compare John 3:19-20 and John 15:2). God's love forgives and cleanses us in order to make us beautiful for Him. In the evening, the task of shedding light is assigned to a lamp, or candle. Similarly, a city only has any value if it serves people: if it is merely a collection of nice houses, streets, walls and buildings, it is of no value. Only as people move into it and establish their lives there does it become worth seeing and do we enjoy a clear view of it. Placed on a hill, a city is easy to see and easy to find, as it derives its value from the ways in which it serves people. The last of the four metaphors Jesus uses is similar. A candle only has any real value if it is placed on a candlestick, where it can serve people by lighting up the room for them.

Each of these four metaphors serves to show us what love is really all about. If you're not sure about this and still wondering whether Jesus is really talking about love here, check the last few verses of Matthew 5. There, Jesus calls on us to love even our enemies - only then will we demonstrate that we are children of God. 'He maketh His sun to rise on the evil and on the good, and sendeth rain on the just and the unjust' (Matt. 5:45). The sunlight and the rain He gives us are vital to both the just and the unjust. He wants us to share our love with everyone, just as He shares light and rain.

Salt, light, a city and a candle all exist for the sake of others. That is what God the Father is like and this is how we can demonstrate that we are His children. Light does not serve itself, but others - just like God does! The great Giver Himself takes a modest place. Just like the sun, whose brightness can't be looked upon, He hides Himself in His serving power. In other words, we can't hold or access or control Him, who is the source of light (1 Tim. 6:16), yet His works cause us and others to worship Him as the Giver of light. Jesus said, 'Let your light so shine before men, that they may see your good works, and glorify your Father which is in heaven' (Matt. 5:16). This should be our starting point for all street work.

The great Giver wishes to be made known through the acts of the little givers. Through us… It's amazing, but true! Our good works don't have to be performed in anonymity. On the contrary. Jesus instructed His disciples to show their own good works to the people around them. 'Oh, she did that and he helped her out. They're Christians; they say they were taught to do that kind of thing by their heavenly Father. He must be a good God. I'd like to get to know Him.' Obviously, we're not called to show off or to put ourselves at the center of attention. Don't go back to living for yourself! If you do, you'll be expecting a reward here on earth rather than from

God (Matt. 6:1). Instead, let all your good works point towards the great Giver of all things. Like the moon reflecting the light of the sun, you can face the great Light and reflect it into the dark places around you.

Avoiding exhaustion

Can we really do all that? Won't we end up exhausted? We may, but if we do, something is wrong. Exhaustion is a wake-up call, telling us to check just how we receive and pass on God's love. Maybe we are trying to pass on things God never gave us. Then our efforts are rooted in ourselves rather than in Him. There's nothing wrong with getting tired, but exhaustion is a signal telling us we've gone too far (Is. 40:29-31). We've neglected to properly apply the fundamental principle of God's Kingdom.

In order to understand this fundamental principle, it might help you to picture three cylinders. The first one has a closed top, the second has a closed bottom and the third one is open both at the top and at the bottom. Each cylinder represents a certain kind of person.

The first one is a person who is not open to God's love. It bounces back off the top. God's blessings may be received, but His love is not; it is denied, deflected, it does not reach the innermost being of this person. So in giving out love to others, this person has to draw on resources within himself. If he does that for a long time, he will end up empty.

The second cylinder is a picture of someone who is open to God's love and allows it to completely fill him. But once this person has been filled, nothing happens anymore, as the bottom of the cylinder is closed. Full is full. There's no room for any more. To this kind of person, the life of faith becomes monotonous. It's the same every day. The fresh stream of God's love becomes a stagnant pool and after a while this person loses interest. In this case, exhaustion results from perhaps wanting to share love, but being afraid of running empty. These people are afraid they might give too much; that others will take advantage of them. Managing this fear of exhaustion takes so much effort that it leads to another kind of exhaustion. Like Cain, these people have begun to live for themselves. This compulsion wears them out.

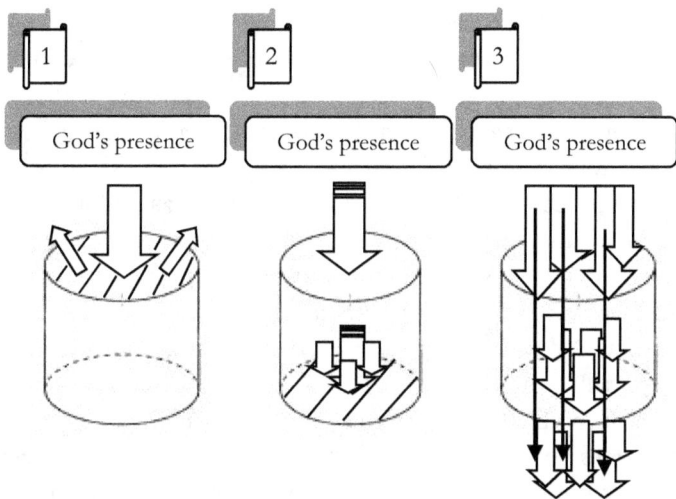

Cylinder 1
This cylinder represents a person with a 'closed top.' He is unable to experience God's presence. His unbelief deflects it.

Cylinder 2
This cylinder represents a person with a 'closed bottom.' He receives God's presence, but because he does not share it with others, it ceases to flow. Stagnant pools soon start to stink. The same thing happens here. The experience of God's blessing goes stale and fades away.

Cylinder 3
This cylinder represents a person who abundantly experiences God's presence. As he passes it on to others through his good works, his 'cylinder' is refilled. A living relationship with God results from this. Sharing God's grace in our connections with other people helps us develop a connection with God in which He shares His grace with us.

Cain did not really want to sacrifice anything. He expected immediate compensation from God for what he did give. One good turn deserves another. He saw that Abel's approach was different. He did not get the response Abel got. Abel did not give something that belonged to him, he gave himself as a person. Cain gave an object, a thing that belonged to him and for which expected some other thing in return. He did not dare to give himself. Yet true sacrifice means giving ourselves. That's what Paul means when he instructs us to give our bodies - that is, everything we are and do - 'as a living sacrifice, holy, acceptable unto God' (Rom. 12:1). Offering miserable gifts from your own strength will exhaust you. You will miss out on the release of letting go and as a result you will not experience that inward refreshing. You will become embittered, because your approach won't work. You will not feel alive inwardly.

Only when you become a person resembling that third cylinder will you be surprised by constant fresh streams of love. You will dare to make real sacrifices. You will be prepared to let go of everything and to trust that God will meet all your needs. As for how or when He does that, you will leave that to Him. The preparedness to give and to pass on will be the decisive factor in your life. As you develop this willingness, you will learn to listen to God's voice telling you when is the right moment to act. And each time you are able to give of yourself, you will rejoice. It's part of the deal (2 Cor. 9:7)! It won't exhaust you, but instead it will renew your strength. And yes, you will be compensated immediately! You'll find that everything you give to others is immediately replenished with a fresh experience of His love. You'll know right away! He will be giving of Himself to you! That is the greatest gift you can receive: God's refreshing streams of love. It will be exciting to keep sharing love. Motivated by this pure love, you'll start taking faith risks. Even if the results don't turn out the way you want them to, you'll know you did it because you love Him. You know what matters - and that

God's foremost interest is in your attitudes and motives. And so you go out into the world with Him.

It really is exciting. It makes you wonderfully dependent on Him and that's just what He wants. It teaches you to live close to Him. In Him and through Him. You'll go out onto the streets. You'll want to share God's love out there.

In Chapter 9, we considered how to use our bodies in connecting with people. In the next chapter, we'll look at how to start conversations and how to connect using words.

11. Talking with people as a street pastor?

Your conversations will be determined by what you have to give

'Sir, may I ask you a question?' The gentleman appeared to be in good spirits. He and his wife were walking and holding hands, enjoying the sunshine. His wife had already noticed they would be passing a group of evangelists. There wasn't much she could do, except to hold her husband's hand a little tighter and hope her husband would get the nonverbal message she was conveying: keep walking! Unfortunately, he slowed down slightly. She gave his arm another little tug. Not too obviously, of course, because that would look rude. Then the question she knew was coming popped out: 'Do you know Jesus?' Seeing that the gentleman had slowed down, a second evangelist jumped forward. He was obviously a veteran, positioning himself in such a way that the couple now had no choice but to stop. This second evangelist started telling them about all the wonderful things that had happened to him since he had gotten to know Jesus: 'My life has changed completely. I can't imagine living without Him anymore.'

The evangelists had now more or less surrounded the couple. You could see the gentleman wishing he had not made the mistake of slowing down. But it was too late. A harsh reaction was not in his nature, so he opted for a tolerant approach, suggesting that each person must decide about these things for himself. 'I'm happy for you, fellows, but when I was a child my parents made me go to church and it meant nothing to me.' The evangelists, grasping the fact that they were dealing with a lost soul, became even more zealous in confronting the gentleman with the consequences of his unbelief. 'But have you ever stopped to consider what will happen to you when you die?' This was a question the gentleman would have preferred to avoid. He offered some more tolerance, but it was a bad move, because it gave the evangelists the feeling they were getting through. 'I already said, I'm really happy for you, fellows. I can really imagine your faith being of great importance to you. Sometimes I wish I had that kind of faith. But I don't.' The lady, meanwhile, was at the point of stepping in and dragging her husband to safety. She hated the aura of superiority that surrounded the two evangelists, as if they were the spiritual champions, and she and her husband were losers.

Sharing blessings

This is how it goes sometimes. I'm not saying this type of evangelism cannot carry God's blessing. I'm sure people have been converted in this way. Nothing is impossible to God. It's a known fact that some people have actually come to a living faith as a result of coercion, manipulation and the promise of earthly benefits. The question, however, is whether the Bible does not show us a different way. Sure, I've stood out there in the marketplace. I've stopped people on the street in a way similar to the scene I described just now. I've knocked on doors. But I always had a feeling there was something wrong about it. I know people who are involved in door-to-door evangelism in poor neighborhoods, and they are blessed with really great openings. People actually come to faith there. The fact that someone is willing to come and visit them and listen to their story just makes them open their hearts. It really can work.

But how did Jesus send out His disciples? They had go out in twos (Matt. 10), which was a way of affirming the truthfulness of their testimony. This doesn't mean we must be rigid about working in twos. Philip appears to have been alone in Samaria and was alone when he spoke with the Ethiopian official (Acts 8). Matthew 10 is about reliability. Perhaps working in twos also offers the possibility of mutual encouragement when things get tough (Eccles. 4:9-10). The disciples were commissioned to share the blessings of the Kingdom (Matt. 10:7-8). This sharing meant proclaiming the Gospel while simultaneously demonstrating the power of the Kingdom. Like heralds, they went out to proclaim the coming of a new era. The time had come for God's blessings and God's presence to be poured out... They proved this with signs. These offered a foretaste of the blessing that was to come when God's presence would be fully manifested.

Dependence on others

While the disciples were given something to share, they were also confronted with their dependence on others. Having been instructed to travel light, they would soon run out of supplies. They would be dependent on the kindness of people they met. They were to avoid the slightest hint that they were the spiritual champions and that everyone else was a failure. The principle of the body was immediately evident: the hand needed the foot. The wandering witness needed someone to offer him a place to sleep. How wise it was of the Spirit to introduce this element of fellowship right at the beginning of these encounters. Note the simplicity of it all, too. Whenever the disciples arrived in a new place, they started by offering a greeting in which the peace of God's Kingdom was conveyed. Then they had to wait and see how this blessing was received. If someone in their audience responded receptively, the disciples were allowed to stay there and share further blessings (Matt. 10:12-13). At the same time, they were allowed to enjoy the love offered to them in the recipient's home.

This is a far cry from how many modern-day evangelists operate. At the very first contact, they dump as many of the Kingdom's blessings as they possibly can on the recipient. More often than not, the recipient - or should I say 'victim?' - is overwhelmed by this bombardment of spiritual riches.

'God changed my life completely! I've witnessed amazing miracles! I always used to be so restless, but now I've found true peace. All my sins have been forgiven. His love is always in my heart. And God has all of this laid up for you, too. Just raise your hands to Him!' And they call this witnessing…

People often say witnessing is all well and good, but it's up to the Spirit to persuade. A recipient will hear a testimony and unbelief will surface: 'It can't be as great as they say it is.' After bombarding the recipient with all the wonderful experiences he has had, the evangelist, seeing unbelief, feels a sense of disappointment. The conversation carries on for a bit, then it comes to an end - occasionally with the evangelist hurling various threats about a future in hell at the recipient. This only makes things worse, of course. The evangelist eventually leaves the recipient with a profound sense of annoyance. I know I'm exaggerating here, but this really is not the way to go about it. It is an approach that does not take into account what the recipient is - and is not yet - ready for. It does not take into account whether there is even the slightest longing for inner peace. No efforts are made to search for a real opening or a way to really connect with this precious human being in a lasting way. There is no exploration of how this other person might be blessed and how his or her treasure chest might gradually be filled at a pace that he or she can cope with. Yet this is how disciples of Jesus should operate. With a sense of mutual dependence.

I already mentioned that Jesus embedded the principle of the Body of Christ in the very first contact. The witness shared a spiritual blessing and the recipient responded by offering a material blessing (Matt. 10:10; 1 Cor. 9:11). Things may not always work this way, but there should be some evidence of giving and receiving. If you see something beautiful in the other person, receive it. Receive every positive response. Every positive desire. And respond to it, even if it does not seem to you to be very spiritual. Whatever good thing you encounter can be a point of lasting connection.

That's how Jesus taught us to work. If there was no response, His disciples were simply to move on, leaving the responsibility for the people they had just visited behind them, the way you might shake dust from your shoes. Jesus does not want His servants to be stressed out. He allows people who have had enough of Him to simply move on. Jesus is interested in seekers. People who hunger and thirst after righteousness (Matt. 5:6). He always takes time out for people like that.

No stress

I mentioned this before when we were considering the New Testament evangelist, but because it is so important, I'd like to say it again. Jesus began to speak in parables because He was looking for seekers of the Kingdom. He concealed the message in parables. Only those really seeking for the truth came to Him to hear the message. They asked Him to explain the meaning and background of the parables. Then they understood what He was getting at. Why? Because it was given to them to understand, and not to others. That's why Jesus hid His message in parables (Matt. 13:10-13).

Jesus does not come along and push His message down everyone's throat! Definitely not! Once He even asked those who stayed behind with Him to leave (John 6:66-67). Jesus went about His work as a pastor in a very relaxed way. He did not rush about feverishly, trying to drag everyone into the Kingdom. Instead, He quietly watched and waited for the people His Father brought to Him (John 6:37-39, 10:29; Heb. 2:13). Those people were everything to Him. With them He founded a united spiritual family (Heb. 2:11). This calls for a pastoral attitude. It calls for speaking with the voice of the Shepherd and watching what happens. The sheep that respond are the Shepherd's sheep. The sheep that do not respond evidently do not belong to the Shepherd (John 10:4-5). It means we can relax. Like the Israelites walking around the city of Jericho in order to conquer it, we must simply go about our business - and watch to see whether the walls begin to crumble. Do what we have to do. You could say we really only have to connect with the people God points out to us through the Spirit. If He doesn't point out anyone - no worries! Jesus didn't worry and fret. Some people will come to faith later. But even that is in God's hands (Gal. 1:15-16). Just quietly carry on and see what God does. Now or later.

Look for places where God can live

Let's say you're a street worker. How would you lead a conversation at a bar?

There are a lot of ways of starting a conversation. It's always good to start on a person-to-person level. When Jesus met the Samaritan woman, He made a comment about being thirsty. He had a plan, but He started with an everyday topic. Seeing a woman with a jar, He simply asked her, 'Ma'am, could you please give Me a drink?' Just like that. It's an example we should follow. Stay focused, but act normal. Look for a personal angle in your contact with other people. Be modest. Jesus expressed His dependence on the woman, even though He had much more to offer than she did. He just approached her as someone in need of her assistance (John 4).

If you're sitting next to someone on a bar stool, you could start by asking something simple, like: 'Do you live near here?'

The answer might be, 'Yeah, I was born and raised here.'

'Do you like it?'

'It's all I know.'

If the other person asks you where you live, you could say you came to the area because of your job. I always have it easy in situations like this, because I simply say I'm a pastor. It's fairly natural to then ask the other person about their beliefs, but I usually hold back on that for a while, preferring to hear some more about the other person's work or personal life, so that God can show me possible points of connection. If you're not a pastor, you could share something about your profession. You could also say you come to the bar or pub because you enjoy meeting people: 'That's why I'm enjoying meeting you here today. I think a good conversation now and then is vital to us humans.' Most people would probably agree with you on that. Your next step could be to share your belief that people have been created for each other, despite the fact that so much goes wrong in that area. 'So much goes wrong in relationships, it's so sad. Do you have good friends?' Often, people will say they do. Whether or not this is really true is something they may not divulge until later on in the conversation. But they'll sense you're not there to engage in small talk. And you can sound out whether they are really interested. If they keep talking, you may be in for great adventure. Meanwhile, keep listening carefully to find out who this person is and how God may be prompting you.

Words spoken by others contain a wealth of wisdom for those who take the time to fathom their depths (Prov. 18:4). Try reading the book of Proverbs and paying special attention to the verses on the use of words; you'll learn a lot and your pastoral work will really benefit. As you carry on listening, some opportunity is likely appear for you to connect: 'Yeah, relationships tend to be hardening these days. But I really believe everything is going to get fixed one day. By God. What are your beliefs?' Most people do not mind you asking personal questions at all, if the timing is right. At least not in my experience. But you can leave the question about beliefs for later, too, if you prefer. In the meantime, carry on your search for the 'prodigal son' in the other person. If you're wondering what you should be looking for in a conversation, here are some pointers:

1. Look for what God is doing in this person's life and connect with it.

2. Look for places where God can live.

This second point is a key element in our search. This may sound strange but tell me, where can God live? He lives with the brokenhearted. The Bible says God has two favorite dwelling places. One is 'the high and holy place' and the other is 'with him that is of a contrite and humble spirit' (Is. 57:15). In these places, He is welcome to manifest who He truly is, the Healer (Is. 57:19). This second place is difficult for us to find, as people do not readily reveal it. It is a place of pain, and we tend to be ashamed of the things it represents. We use a lot of words and jokes to cover up those spots in our lives!

One effective way of covering up our places of inner brokenness is to pose theological or other problems. That's what the Samaritan woman did when Jesus started getting a little too close for comfort (John 4:20). These places of brokenness are where the prodigal son in us hides out. He's sitting there, feeling worth less than the pigs. He doesn't want to be seen there. None of us likes exposing our brokenness. If you're a good listener, you will sometimes sense you are getting close to one of the places. Asking the right questions is more important than offering the right answers. Answers tend to trigger debate, which leads away from brokenness.

If you're in pastoral work, you need to practice asking questions and waiting for the answers the Spirit gives the person you're talking with. Often, their replies will confirm important truths. 'You're right. People really can let you down. What we need is faithfulness!' By affirming statements that are in line with God's truths, you will reinforce those truths in the minds of the people you're talking with.

Of course, this also means you must listen carefully to what remains unspoken. For instance, if you ask someone whether his family lives in the same town as he does and he responds with a laugh, saying, 'Oh, I have my friends here, that's enough for me,' you will know you've touched on a sensitive issue. If you ask someone about his job and he doesn't seem to want to talk about it, you're probably close to the brokenness of a prodigal son. The pain he or she is trying to cover up with silence reveals a place of brokenness or loss in his or her past - in other words, a place of potential change. But change will not happen just like that.

In Isaiah, we read that God lives 'with him that is of a contrite and humble spirit.' Humility is a prerequisite. A person lacking humility may flare up in anger or wallow in self-pity at the thought of brokenness. This means there is still a spirit of rebellion within him. And that spirit has to go. Only when humility enters in, will there be room for God to dwell within that person. In other words, having identified the place of the prodigal son in another person's heart does not mean you're finished. The prodigal son may resist the idea of needing a father. He must have the willingness to 'arise and go' to his father in humility (Luke 15:18).

A good way of helping that other person to take that difficult step is by placing yourself next to him as one more prodigal son. Be a prodigal son to him yourself, share your own brokenness with the brokenhearted, so that you 'might by all means save some' (1 Cor. 9:22). Confessing sins together will open the way to healing (James 5:16). When you share your brokenness, do it with humility. Make sure you don't make yourself the center of attention. In all wisdom, search for hope-giving words. For example, you could share how God has helped you. That will give hope: what worked for you may also work for the other person. Share the story of how your brokenness led you to the Healer.

Conversational techniques

If you're involved in pastoral work, including street work, it's a good idea to get some practice in conversational techniques. That way you will learn to help people open up by asking good questions. It really helps! There is a 'but,' however. Some promoters of conversational techniques do not believe in absolute truth and will tell you to avoid leading a conversation towards 'your' truth. But the Bible tells us Jesus is the truth. Questions about the truth cannot be avoided!

It's not about being right

If He dwells in us with His Spirit, the truth lives within us. Now truth is not the sum total of certain confessions, but rather the presence of the Person who is the truth. He must be found in us, in His steadfastness and trustworthiness. And He can be found in us - in the places of our brokenness! Broken people don't have pretensions. They no longer need to be right all the time. But He is there: trustworthy and steadfast! So in our conversations, we must look for the brokenness in other people. For the person who longs to connect with the Person who is the truth. Only then can healing and eternal life enter in. The truth itself will show the way. There will be no need for arguing.

I often hear conversations centering on a battle against what is negative about the other person: 'Because I don't agree with that.' The result is that the other person usually starts disagreeing with you on more and more things. Focusing on what is positive and using that to get alongside the other person is a way of establishing truth. If someone says to you, 'I think Christians are such hypocrites,' you can argue that it's not all that bad, but you will be taking the position of an opponent. It won't help. But you do know that you've approached a sensitive spot: the other person has evidently experienced hypocrisy. So what you need to do instead of arguing is to find out what caused the pain and how bad the wound is. Even being cautious and saying most people are hypocritical will probably trigger a debate. At least it won't change the other person's view that Christians are especially hypocritical. So instead look for a positive angle. Maybe you could say you appreciate his desire for sincerity.

That way, you will have affirmed a godly quality. Maybe you can ask whether he struggles to be sincere in this world himself: 'There's so much hypocrisy, don't you struggle to be sincere all the time?' By saying something like this, you will have established that this world is in bondage to corruption (2 Pet. 2:18-19.) Maybe this person will tell you when and how he was cheated by hypocrisy. You don't have to open the floodgates of heaven and salvation and the grace of Christ just yet. Encouraging some sensitivity to the need for salvation is already quite a step forward. Some sheep have to get used to the voice of the Good Shepherd. It's okay if this takes time. The first thing to do is to establish whether this person has the spirit of a sheep or of a goat (Matt. 25:32-33).

You can only do this to a certain degree; the final judgment of a person's spirit is God's, and God's alone. But if someone has the spirit of a goat, he or she will keep resisting you, both in words and in actions. At times you may appear to have found an opening, but it won't lead to anything. In dealing with a goat, you can exhaust yourself trying to overcome his stubbornness, but exhaustion is not meant to be a part of pastoral work. Asking the right questions at the right moment, on the other hand, will add depth and meaning to the conversation. As you go about this, don't attack the other person by feverishly throwing biblical truths at them. Instead, carefully explore and examine the best possible angle. Listen and wait for God to give you the right opening. Learning to listen will open up many possibilities for connecting with people. Just make sure you always treat people respectfully. If someone talks to me about making a lot of money, I like to reply with this question, 'Do you really think money makes people happy?' The answer is usually easy to predict: 'No, but it sure makes life a lot easier.'

'So you think a life of ease will make you happy? What about someone who pours himself into something and overcomes a lot of challenges in order to succeed? Nothing easy about that! But don't you think that person might be a lot happier than someone who succeeds without any effort? Besides, how would you define happiness? Or love? In my view, God is love. Does that sound crazy to you?'

Often, I find myself asking questions all the time. I like to try and make people think. God can do a lot in people's lives through the questions we ask. It's similar to what the Israelites did when they marched around the city of Jericho. Only God can cause the walls to crumble. But a few well aimed questions can certainly help. God can use them to dismantle the walls of the heart.

Referring to a higher meaning

You might get into a conversation about a hobby. If people are excited about something, the best way of connecting with them is to get them to tell you all about it. Maybe you could go with them to see what they're so excited about. And you can affirm whatever is good and godly in what they are doing. If you do, you will be connecting the object of that person's love with God, the Giver of true love. It is often a special moment that leads the other person into a whole new realm of thought. The notion that God wants them to enjoy themselves and wants to be a part of it often takes people by surprise. If a person notices that your interest is sincere, they will often start showing an interest in what makes you tick. Sometimes, there are fun parallels to be drawn. After all, the things of this earth ultimately all foreshadow to the eternal things of God. Earthly beauty hints at heavenly beauty. Things growing on earth remind us of the growth of God's Kingdom. Struggles on earth are a reference to the battle raging in the heavenly realm. Destruction on earth exemplifies the destruction of the realm of the devil. Art may serve to remind us of the work of the eternal Artist. Let's say this other person likes working with water colors. Take time to look at his paintings. It's a form of listening, not to his words, but to his work. Then, at the right moment, you could say God is an Artist, maybe like this, 'You know, just now you were talking about the struggles in your life. And here you are painting. Well, it strikes me that some wet streak of color may at one point look ridiculous, but with another stroke of the brush here and another touch there, it suddenly turns into a landscape. Don't you think that may be how God is at work in your life? You can't see what it means just yet. But just trust the Artist.'

Once there is a basis of mutual trust and you've had a couple of good conversations, you might invite this other person to join a group you feel he or she may fit into. In a group, more connections are made than you can ever accomplish on your own. And the more connections there are drawing this person towards God, the easier it is for God to create space for faith and change.

We'll be getting back to the importance of groups in the next section, when we take a more practical look at different ways of getting connected with people. When Christians get together, communities are born - communities of broken people who have found their Healer.

Sadly, the church often gives the impression it is meant only for perfect people. But Jesus intended the church for sinners.

If you want to connect with people, it's like setting out on a journey - a journey which we know can only be completed prayerfully. God Himself will have to show you the way. And He will probably give you other openings than the ones He has given me.

Appendix 2 offers thirteen points of attention I like to share with participants in our Discipleship School. They cover the material we have discussed in this chapter as well as some additional issues.

We are called to connect. Looking for points of connection should be our starting point. Opportunities to bind up people's wounds, first, and, second, to become bound up with people's lives ourselves, in terms of relationships. Just to be on the safe side, I'd like to share a brief study of the Book of Acts in relation to this subject. It is the final part of this section of the book on my vision. The question at the center of our study will be this: Does the Book of Acts reveal lines of thought and action similar to the ones we have discussed here, or does it suggest our approach may be entirely off track?

12. What can we learn from the book of Acts?

A brief study on the Book of Acts

Luke wrote the Book of Acts as a sequel to his gospel. He says the gospel is a report of the initial acts performed by Jesus on earth. His second book picks up where the first one leaves off (Acts 1:1). In other words, the Book of Acts is about the acts of Jesus. Jesus uses His Body to perform these acts, that is, the group of believers that came into existence around the apostles. This is a vital piece of information. The characteristics of Jesus' work before His ascension recur later in the acts of the apostles and are meant to be visible in the churches. Including ours.

Jesus proclaimed the Kingdom of God was near - so near, you could touch it. Then He demonstrated it through His deeds. He was the coming King of this Kingdom (Matt. 21:38), but He did not go around showing off about it. He often told others not to speak about it (Mark 3:12; 8:30; 9:9). So Jesus' acts were proof of His special identity (John 5:19-20). These acts provoked hostility from His opponents (John 5:18). His impressive acts led to further testimonies of His identity (John 5:24), although the fullness of His identity was not yet revealed. This was the pattern: acts/testimonies - resistance - further testimonies/acts. You could say that the testimonies about Jesus' identity often followed reactions - or resistance - to His acts. His acts were aimed at needy sinners (John 5:14).

So what do we see when we look at Jesus? First, we see the wonderful acts of the Kingdom (John 9:30-33); second, we see Him slandered (John 8:45-51); third, we see His special connection with seeking sinners (Matt. 9:11-13).

This connection with seeking sinners had already been announced prior to His life on earth (Is. 53:5-6). Testifying about Jesus on the basis of the first and the third point mentioned above - Jesus' acts and His connectedness -

resonates with the vision presented in this book. Obviously, you don't have to go looking for the second point - slander - to be a witness, but if it happens, you know God can use it.

We should recognize a similar pattern in the acts of Jesus' followers. Let me sum up once more the reasons there are for witnessing. I'll list them in random order, but if there is a fixed order, we will have to take it into account. What matters is that in our own vision, witnessing has the same place as it had in Jesus' day. That means it should be based on our seeking to connect (1) through caring (2) and through relationships.

Acts

Which occasions for witnessing should we expect to see in the Book of Acts?

1. Special events, such as miracles and unusual outpourings of blessing. I like to call this the binding up of wounds, or practical caring. These are acts in which God's love flows through us to others.
2. Persecution, slander or other evil reactions.
3. Things God has done previously in people's lives. I like to refer to this as becoming bound up with other people in relationships. This is how the early church connected with seeking sinners.

In Acts 2, we read about the outpouring of the Holy Spirit. This special event paved the way for Peter's sermon. A miracle occurred and through that miracle blessings were poured out. The miracle itself was preceded by prayer. A hundred and twenty people had spent ten days praying intensively that they might be a blessing to the world (Acts 1:14). Jesus Himself had told them to wait prayerfully (Acts 1:8). The power of the Kingdom would then appear - the same healing power as Jesus had demonstrated on earth. The interaction is immediately evident here: Jesus is acting through people. After ten days, a sound like a rushing wind was heard on the streets of Jerusalem. Eager to find out what was going on, people made their way to the house where the sound had been heard. I imagine the hundred and twenty people inside now came out onto the street.

Then another surprise took place. The believers were heard speaking languages and dialects they had never learned. They spoke about God's work in a way that pierced the hearts of those listening. Peter called this kind of speaking prophetic. In the pastoral sense, many wounds were no doubt bound up. And perhaps this event would have stopped there, going no further than a very personal encouragement session, but then resistance arose. Mockers began to challenge Peter, saying, 'Listen to that! Their strange babbling is simply the result of too much wine!' There are two openings for witnessing here: a special event has occurred (1) and the believers are being slandered (2).

Later, more unusual events took place causing tongues to wag about the gospel (Acts 2:43-47). In a short time, many people came to faith.

In Acts 3 and 4, we see the same combination of miracles and persecution. Chapter 3 offers a very stark example. A lame man's wounds are not just bound up, they are completely healed and he enters 'into the temple walking, and leaping and praising God' (Acts 3:8). Peter and John then explain to the bystanders that this is the work of Jesus. After which they are arrested (Acts 4). This 'forced' them to share even more about the One they were following. This persecution led to further blessing and an increased desire to share.

When Ananias and Sapphira appeared on the scene, things went wrong. The sudden deaths of these two people had a purging effect on the church, and released still more power. From all over the area, people began to bring the sick and those oppressed by evil spirits. Their spiritual and physical wounds were bound up and many were healed (Acts 5:16). The result? More persecution. Arrest followed. Stephen was stoned - an event that provided an occasion for an incredible sermon. The persecution forced many Christians to move away, with some settling in Samaria. Due to previous events, there was already a certain degree of receptiveness to the work of God among the despised Samaritans. Those spreading the gospel were able to connect with that (3). When their message was confirmed by miracles, problems arose with a man called Simon the Sorcerer. But the principle of connecting with what God had already been doing worked well here (Acts 8:6-13). It's also visible in the story of that lone traveler who was interested in God's work among the Jews. Connecting with what God was doing in the heart of this seeking sinner, Philip was able to plainly present the gospel to the Ethiopian official (Acts 8:30).

New connections

A whole new phase in the work of Jesus was ushered in when Paul was forced to recognize His Savior as Lord (Acts 9). Before Paul was sent out to preach the gospel to the Gentiles, Jesus caused a breakthrough in Peter's life. Being the leader of the first church, Peter had a threshold to cross. He had to find out whether it was alright to connect with Gentiles. So he was told that the road to the uncircumcised was open. Jesus made him visit a gentile called Cornelius. What a challenge it was to Peter, a Jew! Much to his surprise, he immediately connected with what Jesus had already been doing in Cornelius' life (Acts 10:47). Peter had some difficulty recognizing that Jesus was already at work in places he himself was as yet unwilling to enter due to his old views. Jesus instructed him through a vision, in which Peter saw 'all manner of fourfooted beasts of the earth, and wild beasts, and creeping things, and fowls of the air.' He was horrified: they were unclean, they could not possibly be connected with

God. But God had declared the creatures clean (Acts 10:15). You see, God was already at work in Cornelius. And it was vital Peter would connect with him - in the way I've been describing in this book: the work of God in other people's lives offers grounds for relating. After this episode, Peter had to go back to the church and explain that God crosses the old, familiar boundaries in seeking new relationships (Acts 11).

There was also a breakthrough in Antioch. Some Greeks suddenly became believers (Acts 11:21). Gentiles... how exciting! But the believers still needed a big push in order to cross the old boundaries. The apostle James was murdered. What a blow to the church! On top of that, Peter was arrested. Herod was trying to gain some votes in Jerusalem, so he came up with a political trick: pester the Christians, please the Jews (Acts 12:2-3). Jerusalem was never going to be the same for the believers. They loved the city of David and were convinced it was to be the center of renewal. Surely, this was the place in which 'the tabernacle of David that is fallen' (Amos 9:11) was to be raised up! It was - but not the way the first believers assumed. First, they had to let go of the familiarity and comfort of Jerusalem.

I sometimes feel that in our day and age, God may also be dislodging people from the safety of the organized church and moving them into areas in which nothing has been organized. As if He may be teaching them new forms of connecting.

This certainly seems to be the case in Acts. The compulsion to go to new countries grew. Note how subtly Jesus led this movement throughout the book of Acts. Step by step, He prepared the way, so that eventually Paul and Barnabas could go out into the world. They were sent (Acts 13).

So which strategy did these missionaries deploy? They looked for places where God had already been at work. For instance, Paul usually went to local synagogues (13:5, 15; 14:1; 17:1, 10, 17; and 18:19). Or to houses of prayer (16:13). These were often visited by Gentiles interested in the God of Israel. Jesus wanted Paul and his friends to meet people who were hungry for salvation. Paul followed a fixed pattern of looking for connections prepared and facilitated by God. Even in Rome his first contacts were with the Jews living there. He wanted to discover how Jesus intended to continue His work in their lives (28:17). When Paul was invited to speak at the Areopagus in Athens, he recognized yet another opportunity to tap into something that was already there (17:19). He found his connection at a heathen altar dedicated to 'the unknown god' (17:23). Paul quoted poetry that would have been familiar to his hearers, as it was from one of their own poets. He recognized an opportunity: in the poet's lines, God had embedded a truth Paul could use (17:28). This openness to what Jesus has done and is still doing in the lives of people of different cultures and backgrounds should be a determining factor in how we move out into the world. This is how conversations with all kinds of people begin.

On the island of Malta, Paul found a point of connection in a miracle of healing (28:8-9). He crossed boundaries to bless people. He bound up their wounds. We may not be able to perform the miracles Paul did. But this brief study of the Book of Acts does show us that the way to get started is by offering practical care.

The two aspects of 'binding' are interwoven

What did we see in the Book of Acts? That the two tenets of our vision of street work are also present in Acts:

1. Practical care and the binding up of wounds;
2. Connecting, or becoming bound up, with what God is doing or has done in the lives of other people.

As you can see, these two kinds of 'binding' are interwoven. It's obvious when you think about it, because that's what

God is like. It's important to be aware of this in our work. So from now on, let's allow these two approaches to intersect.

In the next section of this book (Chapters 13 through 17), I'd like to take a closer look at the practicalities of binding wounds and becoming bound up with people. We'll be discussing both approaches without always differentiating between the two, simply because we have now seen that they are, in fact, inseparable.

Possibilities for connecting
(Chapters 13-17)

Chapters 13 through 17 are all about the different possibilities for connecting with other people. In our brief study of the Book of Acts, we saw that even resistance can provide an occasion for witnessing. As most of us do not like resistance, we're going to look first at how we can overcome our fear of resistance.

13. What practical steps can you take towards caregiving?

Demonstrate real love by overcoming your fears

Jesus did not talk about love, everything about Him *was* love: everything He said, did, and didn't say or do. He was love when He embraced and when He rebuked, in joy and in sorrow. His entire existence radiated love. He couldn't help expressing His practical love to all people in the most tangible ways (Matt. 5:44-48). It was His way of speaking with the voice of the Shepherd. And having spoken, He would then wait and see who would come forward and join Him as His sheep (John 6:37). Whoever came to Him knew he had been called by name (John 10:3). His sheep just know. Love that is not felt is empty. His performance of real Kingdom acts gave the King His true face (John 5:36). And when we meet Him face to face, the issue will be real acts of love, as we are confronted with what we did, or did not, do out of love for Him (Matt. 25:31-46).

James wrote that 'faith without works is dead' (James 2:26). In street work, especially, authenticity in love is indispensable. Authenticity only shows when there is total commitment. Jesus went the whole way. In doing so, He gave us an example to follow (John 15:12-13). Maybe one reason things often go wrong is that as church folk we tend to think love is some kind of holy feeling. But when Jesus washed His disciples' feet, it was an act of love. When He hung bleeding and gasping for breath on the cross, that was an act of love, too. Perhaps our tendency to think of love as some pious feeling has to do with our misunderstanding of the parable of the talents (Matt. 25:14-30). What is meant by a 'talent' in this story?

Use your talents

When we hear the word 'talent,' we normally think of something special or out of the ordinary: 'He has such a talent for drawing,' or 'She is such a talented singer.' But in Matthew 25, the word 'talent' is not meant this way. Rather, it refers to the whole package of possibilities you received along when you were given the gift of life. Your time, your money, your ovum or sperm cell, your clothes, your home and all your capabilities and opportunities. The idea is that you are to use all of this as the One Who gave it to you intended it to be used.

There are different talents. The first servant received five talents, the second two and the last just one talent. We are not to read any kind of restriction or limitation into these numbers - they simply represent the whole of life's possibilities, with some having more and others fewer. This totality of possibilities is what we must learn to put to use. The moment a carpenter recognizes that his carpentry skills are part of this wider package of talents, he will suddenly understand that he can be a blessing in many different ways by using his talent for the Kingdom. He may not be able to perform miracles, but as he learns to go about doing jobs in love and in the name of the great Carpenter, Jesus, he will be spreading the works of the Kingdom wherever he goes, to the honor of the King. The more faithful he is, the more God's Spirit will give to others through him. And who knows, he may yet perform miracles, as this is what is promised to faithful followers of the King (Matt. 25:29). If every Christian started using his or her talents for the Kingdom, the result would be a massive street work movement. Like in the days of the first church, when everyone put his talents to use in building up the Kingdom. No one in those days said that 'ought of the things which he possessed was his own' (Acts 4:32). As we take on this attitude, Christians will once again be known as people who are always willing to lend a helping hand. It would be an answer to that prayer, 'Thy Kingdom come!' We pray this so easily, but Jesus wants to make it reality through our talents. Our time is His. Our hobbies are His, as are the skills we've received for earning our daily bread. Even our enjoyment belongs to Him!

Sacrifice with love

This is why Paul encourages us to give abundantly and cheerfully (2 Cor. 9:6-9). We are called to be sincere priests, sacrificing to Him our entire lives and everything that is part of our lives (Rom. 12:1). You can imagine what a bad impression it would have made if the Old Testament priests serving in the temple had gone about their work grudgingly. Just picture their long faces: 'Oh, no, here comes another stupid sinner. We're going to have to slaughter another goat. And the goats are so stubborn. Let me check if this one is without blemish. Not that it makes much sense: the people have such sensitive consciences that they wouldn't dream of bringing an imperfect sacrifice. And even if they did, it would be their problem, not mine. They want to risk facing God's wrath? It's their business. Anyway, here's the knife, better get this nasty job done. Hope I don't get too much blood on my clothes, or worse, in my face.' If someone were to do the work of a priest like that, the temple would soon lose its respectability. God certainly does not want this kind of service. We are the New Testament priests, called to sacrifice to God continually and in many ways. If we do not sacrifice in love, chances are we will defile our high calling. God works through love. Love sets things in motion. If we gave away everything we had, sacrificing our very bodies, but did it without sincere love, it would have no meaning at all (1 Cor. 13:3). At the same time, I can also imagine us bringing sacrifices for which we have to overcome fears. It's quite normal to experience an inward struggle about something, while deliberately and wholeheartedly deciding to go through with it. Just before the crucifixion, Jesus had to face His fears (Heb. 5:7-10). We may be afraid to perform acts of obedience, but we must never give in to this fear. People who allow that to happen are 'fearful, and unbelieving' and do not belong in the heavenly Jerusalem (Rev. 21:8).

Cross thresholds

On November 9, 2001, I first started visiting bars and pubs in Sliedrecht. I was awfully nervous - perhaps in part because I had chosen a bar that had always made me feel uneasy. From the outside, you could just feel how closed this place was to the Light of God. To this very day, it is the most difficult bar for me to visit. But one night, I decided the time had come and I headed out. When I reached the place, I walked on down the street. My conscience disagreed violently. 'What are you doing? You wimp, you purposely walked right on past the place! First you prayed God would come with you and now you don't dare? Go back, you coward!' I obeyed. Somewhat dazed, I placed my hand on the door knob and pushed. I pushed some more. The door wouldn't open. I looked around. I felt so stupid! But nobody was watching. Then I tried another door. Oops - I hadn't looked properly to see which door was the entrance to the bar! The second door opened and I stepped inside. The air was thick with smoke. I tried to offer a greeting. The guy behind the bar offered me a forced nod. My throat felt like sandpaper. I wasn't really thirsty, but I thought maybe a beer would help. It didn't.

I took a stool at the bar. Across from me, a bunch of deadpan faces were staring at me without quite staring at me. I felt like a total zero in their company and told myself to try and act relaxed. So I walked over to the wall to take a look at some of the pictures. There were symbols of Feyenoord, Rotterdam pro soccer club, and a few other clubs somehow connected to the bar.

> Jesus said the fields 'are white already to harvest' (John 4:35). We often have a hard time recognizing that. Maybe we don't go out into the fields enough?

Just then another guy stepped into the bar. It didn't take long for me to see that he was not one of the regulars. He sat down and drank a beer, but like me, he did not seem to feel quite at ease. When his glass was half empty, I offered him a beer, asking him whether he was from Sliedrecht. 'No, thank goodness! What a lousy town this is! I came here for my son, but I sure regret it. That pious-looking Reformed crowd, they're terrible, especially on Sundays. Nobody even greets you. It really annoys me.'

I had thought the regulars sitting at the bar were a bunch of tough nuts to crack, but it turned out there was a worse set of people in town: the Reformed Christians! That's what this fellow had said. It was not encouraging.

He went on to vent his anger at our deceased prime minister, Den Uyl. And then there was another person on his hit list. He said he had a pistol at home and was ready to put a bullet in that person's head. I tried not to let on that my hopes for a meaningful conversation had dropped below zero. He went on and on, complaining about Sliedrecht all the way through, repeating again and again how lousy this town of Reformed Bible-believers really was. Then he asked me if I lived in Sliedrecht myself and how I had wound up here. I sighed and laughed as if I was about to crack a joke. Then I said, 'You really don't want to know how I got here!'
'Why not? Come one, tell me!'
I had aroused his curiosity. Unfortunately...
'If I tell you, you won't want to drink that beer I gave you.'
Now he was laughing, too. And getting more curious every second. 'Yeah, right. Come on, it can't be that bad.'

I took that as a hint that perhaps he had seen something in me that he liked and decided to out the truth. 'I'm a Reformed pastor!'
'No! That's impossible, you're kidding me!'
I put my hand in my inside pocket and pulled out a pocket Bible.

He still wasn't convinced, but it did cost him some of his self-assurance. His attitude changed. He even started calling me 'sir!' What's more, he began to ask some serious questions. I was able to tell him what I was doing in the bar and to talk to him about the love of Jesus. So far, he has kept

Jesus at a distance, but I still visit him at his home a couple of times a year.

I had to overcome my fear. Later that evening, when I was back in the safety of my own home, I was immensely grateful for having been able to cross that daunting, but crucial threshold.

Don't be overcome by fear

I still have a threshold to cross every time I enter a bar late at night. You never know what you're going to encounter. The bar I described above is still daunting to me. I have it from insiders that certain individuals in there are happier to see me leave than to see me come. I've always felt it, but actually hearing it makes the walk to that bar a lot harder.

I remember a conversation I once had in another bar. No sooner had we started talking than someone else came to join us. He gave me one long, withering look. Then he left. The person I was talking to commented dryly, 'Yeah, that guy really doesn't like you.'

There's another pub I more or less consider my home base. It's where our monthly church services are held. Once I walked in there and hit a raging storm. A visitor who was quite antagonistic towards Christianity started heaping the sins of the church on me, with loud cursing and swearing. We were a bunch of dirty pedophiles! At first I sat down at some distance, but he just went on and on, and after some time I got up and left. Later, some of the other folks who had been there told me they felt terrible about what had happened. I just laughed it off and pretended it hadn't bothered me. But I sure knew I would need to say an extra prayer to overcome my fears next time around.

In those days, there were three bars in which I sensed a degree of hostility. A couple of months later I was standing near the entrance to a fourth bar, talking to some people. They were telling me they had stopped smoking pot and using cocaine. Great news. Then a young fellow came and stood right next to me and said, 'Are you that church guy?' I didn't quite understand, because of his slur. Angered, he repeated, 'Are you that Christian?' I gathered he had heard about me. So with a smile I pleaded guilty, hoping it might break the ice. It didn't. Instead, he walked off muttering obscenities and saying, 'Just remember I do not like you. I hate you!'

If you've had a couple of responses like that one, it's not easy to hit the streets at night. I know I'm in this work for God, otherwise I couldn't do it. Whenever I walk into a bar, I can feel the tension. But whenever I decide to stay home, I feel even more restless, because I know I need to be out there. The idea that nobody is really interested in me or in my message is constantly gnawing at my heart.

Sometimes, people *are* eager to listen. I found that out in June, 2011. I was tired after several busy months. The week before I had been cursed and yelled at by that young man who had asked if I was 'that church guy.' I was bone-weary. Still, deciding not to give in to my fears, I headed out for the one bar in which I had felt the fiercest resistance. I stepped inside and found a stool at the corner of the bar. Two men sitting at the opposite corner had me in full view and seemed to be enjoying that fact. One of them got up to go somewhere, and within minutes the second made contact with me. I had not seen him before. When I happened to mention my first name, his eyes nearly popped out. 'You're Gerard Vrooland? The pastor? I've heard so much about you, I'm really glad to meet you. I've always wanted to talk to you. I'm really searching.' I could hardly believe my ears. I jotted down his phone number in order to meet him the following week. He found the way back to his Savior.

Not much later, another man offered me a beer right out of the blue. He wanted to talk to me as well. Another phone number, another meeting. 'Thank you, Lord!'

These things really happen. In fact, I rarely return home disappointed. Almost every time, there are meaningful conversations and opportunities to speak freely about Jesus. And even if I have not had a great conversation, I've been there, people have seen me and I've quietly prayed for them.

Learn to love thresholds

Lately, I've been seeking out new thresholds. I find they strengthen my faith. You could say I've more or less started to love thresholds. Crossing a threshold means you have a passionate desire for God's presence. During my night-time exploits, I always carry a little cross in one of my pockets. As I move about, I hold on to it as if I'm holding hands with Jesus. I tell myself, 'He is with me. He has given me all things. He will give me strength. He loves me. He is seeking the people I am about to meet. He knows who will find Him.' That is the blessing of high thresholds: they force you to stay close to the Savior in order to overcome your fears. Jesus did it, too (Heb. 5:7-8). So recently I contacted a mosque and started some conversations there about Jesus. I have this inner drive and I am beginning to love that drive. It can cause some great thrills! Some folks go bungee jumping to get a thrill, but I prefer this thrill! It forces me to take so many hurdles with Him. It makes me feel small and dependent on God. In and of myself, I'm way too frightened, but with Him I have the courage. And it works! 'By my God have I leaped over a wall' (Ps. 18:30).

A lot of people get addicted to certain kicks: the kick of smoking a joint, the kick of a trip, of buying stuff, gossiping, playing poker, having sex et cetera. I believe this is Satan using a mechanism intended for God. Satan uses the drive, the tension and the kick that follows. But God wants to give us a faith kick! He called Noah to build an ark, Abraham to sacrifice his son, Gideon to beat a vast army with just three hundred men, David to slay Goliath with no more than a sling and a stone, the frightened disciples to travel to unknown peoples and make them into disciples of Jesus.

The devil stole the kick mechanism from God, but we can take it back and have adventures with God! It's God's prerogative to have adventures with people, not the devil's! God wants us to get our kicks with Him! He wants us to start loving thresholds! As we cross them, people who have a deep-seated dislike of the gospel may not react positively. Yet in my experience, most of them respect the fact that we cross boundaries and look for people in places where we are not expected. Gaining respect in this way, I suppose, is a form of witnessing. Glory to God!

We saw in Acts that binding up wounds and connecting through relationships are interwoven. So, in the next chapter, I'd like to look at how these connections come into being.

14. How do connections come about?

Examples of love and creativity

In this chapter, I'd like to share some examples of connections. I'll be letting go of the distinction between connections made by binding up wounds and those made through the development of relationships, as the two are so closely interlinked. Obviously, the examples we'll be looking at could be extended with endless variations. What I would like is to encourage a new flexibility in thinking in terms of possibilities for practically blessing other people. In order to share God's love with others in ways they will really notice, we have to identify their real needs. Sharing God's love will then have a healing effect; it will heal wounds and connect people to God and to each other.

Building 33 was launched, because we saw a real need among young people. It was started as an attempt to help them avoid getting wounded while hanging around, or living, on the streets. We wanted our center to be a place where we could bind up wounds, in hopes of developing relationships with young people in that way. In launching an initiative like ours, you shouldn't expect immediate waves of conversions. Your goal should be to provide a means through which young people can be exposed to God's work. The fact that they do not always recognize God's presence should not hinder us from doing the work. Do what God does. He causes the sun to rise on the evil and the good, without distinction (Matt. 5:45). Likewise, we must look for ways of allowing God's light to shine on people, to bless them.

Use your hands

I met Riet[8] on the annual Dutch celebration of the Queen's birthday in April. She started talking about her stranded

---

[8] Pronounce as 'Reet.'

relationship and how violent her partner had been. She told me how angry she had been at him - and at the police for not protecting her. Now I was out enjoying the royal festivities with Carolien and we kept getting stopped by people who wanted to ask how we were doing. So it wasn't a good place for a long conversation. I pulled out my diary.

A couple of weeks later I was at her place for coffee. She seemed more cheerful now and told me someone had given her a children's Bible, which she had been reading now and then. I suspect she was saying this mainly to please the pastor; her faith, I found out during subsequent visits, had the depth of a scratch on a record. Every time I came by, she told me the same thing. I hoped it was a sign of latent faith, especially as I was able to pray with her a few times. But as winter set in, it all disappeared. Her anger came back sevenfold. She was furious at her ex. But now she was also mad at the mayor, who had provided her with new housing. She started blaming the housing corporation for the fact that Sliedrecht was showing signs of dilapidation. The corporation had done nothing, she said, to fix things. It was a crying shame. She may have been right, actually, because her apartment was drafty and there was a damp odor about the place that could have given anybody acute rheumatism. Which, as a matter of fact, she had. I felt perhaps prayer was needed here. But I was wrong. 'Prayer? Oh, come on! I don't believe that stuff!' I uttered a quiet sigh. Then she showed how her ex had left the kitchen. 'He promised me he'd fix it up, but look at it...' I looked and saw the bare cement of the walls. I could hear the wind whistling under the door. I saw various disconnected kitchen appliances. It seemed impossible to cook a meal in here. Scratching my head, I thought to myself, 'What good is a pastor to this woman? What she needs right now is not someone who will just fold his hands with her, but a guy willing to get his hands dirty around here!'

That Sunday I used the situation I had encountered as an example in my sermon. There were a lot of people in church that morning who did not belong to our congregation. After the service, two of these guests stood waiting for me. They told me they were handymen and really wanted to help. I was so excited I mentioned their initiative in my column in the local newspaper. Riet's faith still has the depth of a table scratch. She has not gotten much further than she was; perhaps I should even say she seems less open than ever to the gospel. But we're called to bind up wounds; we're not responsible for the results. My account in the newspaper of the help offered by our two guests was read by a lot of people, to the honor of God. The story, like many others, passed from mouth to mouth. Jesus said, 'Let your light so shine before men, that they may see your good works, and glorify your Father which is in heaven' (Matt. 5:16).

Exposition 2 - The binding agent is serving: Matthew 20:20-28

The binding agent in God's Kingdom is loving service. The more you realize we are dealing with two separate realms, the more you'll understand the importance of this kind of service. The two realms are built on entirely opposite principles. The first is the Kingdom of God, which is built on offering service; the second is the realm of the devil, which is built on being served. You might say the Kingdom of God has the shape of an upside down pyramid, while the devil's pyramid stands upright. It's up to us to choose which pyramid we want to get involved in.

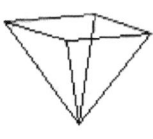　　　　　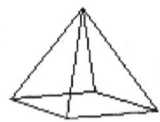

God　　　　　　　　　　　　　　

God lovingly supports　　　　The devil demands the support
everyone and everything　　　　of everyone and everything

The binding agent in God's Kingdom is service (Matt. 20)

1. The mother of the sons of Zebedee wanted her sons to rule (Matt. 20:21). Her request caused a quarrel among the disciples (Matt. 20:24).
2. Jesus pointed out that her request matched the principles of the realm of the devil, where rulers 'exercise dominion' over their subjects (Matt. 20:25).
3. He taught His disciples that being great in God's Kingdom means giving your life to serve others. 'Whosoever will be chief among you, let him be your servant' (Matt. 20:27).

This means we're caught up in a spiritual battle, because by nature we don't want to serve!

Practicing perseverance in service

If you want to be of real value in God's Kingdom, you have to practice humility (Matt. 11:29), service (Matt. 20:25-28) and perseverance (Matt. 24:13).

We serve because God serves and we have received His Spirit!

Gen. 2:18: 'I will make him an help meet for him' (the woman is given a place of honor!).

Gen. 4:1: '(...) I have gotten a man from the Lord.'
We often read in the Bible that the Lord is a Helper (2 Chron. 20:9; 32:8; Ps. 37:40 et cetera).

He gives Himself - He sends forth His Spirit 'and they are created' (Ps. 104:30).

The devil, however, is a thief who comes 'to steal, and to kill, and to destroy' (John 10:10).

God overcomes evil with good, but never by force!

He is always just. That's why He paid for our sins. It's how He overcame evil. People who refuse God's payment have to pay for their own sin. That is justice!

Our lives as God's children are covered by Him Who paid for us (the Lamb's book of life). Whoever insists on paying himself, is given a book of life of his own (Rev. 20:11-15).

God serves, but never forces anything on anyone. We are free to reject His service.

'He maketh His sun to rise on the evil and on the good' (Matt. 5:45)

He cares about all people, and judges without respect of persons (Mal. 1:11; 1 Pet. 1:17).

But He does appeal to His people on account of their position (Mal. 1:6; Matt. 11:2-24).

He will keep serving until the measure of sin of the suffering of His children has been filled (Noah, Sodom and Gomorrah, Canaan, Jerusalem, Revelation).

God will keep serving until there is no service left to perform!

When there is no service left to perform, God's help will consist in destroying all evil, so that its influence will remain limited (Ps. 125:3). But He has 'no pleasure in the death of the wicked' (Ezek. 33:11).

He will determine the time of judgment (Acts 1:7), but He will allow Himself to be influenced

When people humble themselves before God, He postpones judgment. The people of Nineveh are an example of this (Jona 3:6-10), and so is Moses (Ex. 33:14-17). See also 2 Kings 21:16 and 2 Kings 22:15-20.

He is particularly influenced by His own lovingkindness, or His name (Ezek. 20:44).

He bestowed grace on the seed of Abraham (Heb. 2:16). In other words, He offered help!

God is constantly serving us through His lovingkindness (Lam. 3:22-23).

Develop this servant attitude and you will have fellowship with Him (Matt. 24:45-47)

End of exposition 2 - The binding agent is serving: Matthew 20:20-28

The threat of homelessness

In the winter of 2010, we saw a problem emerging for a man called Co. I had been visiting Co for some time in the apartment he had been living in. He and his friends had a pretty tough reputation in the drugs scene. We watched films about the Bible at his place, along with a friend of his. Then we would talk about what we had seen. Those were beautiful moments. I could see those two men gradually opening up to the gospel.

That winter it was terribly cold and Co's apartment was not heated. Then I heard he'd been told to move out. Carolien and I both knew this meant we would have to offer him a place in our own home. We hoped and prayed some other place would be found. We were pretty busy. If Co moved in, the peace and quiet of our own home would be ruined. In the end, a fellow-believer kindly offered us the use of an apartment. This place did need some cleaning, some decorating and some furniture. We called on our supporters and soon the apartment was a picture of coziness. It was ready for Co to move in.

Meanwhile, it turned out Co had lost his ID, which meant he was no longer eligible for a welfare benefit. As far as the Dutch state was concerned, he did not exist. Carolien tackled this problem, and a few months later Co's life, at least as a Dutch citizen, had been totally transformed. All his friends and acquaintances heard about the change. Today, we get together with Co and six of his friends at his apartment to talk about the Bible. On Sunday, June 19, 2011, Co was baptized. Thanks be to God!

Contact with the outside world

Eef[9] is another person we've been able to serve. Eef spends his days at home, killing time by making boxes full of beautiful postcards, greeting cards and bookmarks. He's also pretty good at glass engraving and a lot of other things - anything to stay home. Day after day, he's busy with his crafts. When I first found out about his life, it seemed to me like a prison.

I set out to find a shop that might be willing to sell his products. An evangelical bookstore allowed him to place a box of bookmarks in their shop and sell them for Building 33. The COTS volunteers made all the arrangements. We're still looking for other sales outlets. The idea is to help Eef get in touch with the outside world. It's good to see him already participating in a small part of God's Kingdom. He enjoys it.

---

[9] Pronounce as 'safe.'

Focusing on a group

These are some real-world examples of concrete care for individuals. There are also many different ways of focusing on certain groups of people. I'm going to list eight pointers that will help you develop a strategy for blessing a group. I've drawn them from lessons we've learned in our work at Building 33 and COTS. You can probably add some more yourself.

What does it take to reach out to a specific group?

1. Always meet with your group at the same time, same place.

Regularity fosters a sense of security. Our young folk know exactly when Building 33 is open to them. Those interested in attending our church service in the pub know it is always held on the first Sunday of the month at a fixed time. At Christmas, we've had to adapt our schedule a few times for the sake of the pub owner; it caused a lot of confusion. People kept asking when the service was scheduled. If people have to think too hard about something, they'll give up more easily. Mind you, I can imagine some activities being held at varying times - but only if you tap into something your group is really passionate about.

Soccer is a great example. When I was a pastor in Doetinchem[10], we tried to imagine what would be the best place to build a church. My favorite spot was right next to the stadium of FC De Graafschap, the local pro soccer club. There's a really neat plaza right next to the stadium and I pictured a church there with coffee tables and chairs outside. My idea was to adapt our church service schedule to the soccer matches: we'd have a simple, one-hour meeting two hours before every match, followed by free coffee. We'd

---

[10] Pronounce as 'Dootinchem' with a hard 'g.'

decorate the indoor coffee area with pictures and symbols of FC De Graafschap to share the language of the people we wanted to reach. Meanwhile, we'd try to develop contacts with soccer fans attending the games, inviting them for a free coffee before every match. Gradually, we would extend our invitation to include the pre-match, pre-coffee church services. That way, we would connect with their passion, and coffee table conversations would introduce them to something far more worthy of our passion: a life with Jesus! Expressing sensitivity to the needs of these people - for instance, by sending a card or dropping in if someone is sick - would only add to the effect. Being flexible as a church for the sake of unbelievers is characteristic of Jesus: He often adapted to human institutions (Matt. 17:24-27). Paul also showed a lot of respect for people's customs (1 Cor. 9:19-23).

Paul wrote about the contents of a worship service. What might seem inconceivable to us became the norm at Corinth: they were instructed to adapt their meetings to unbelieving guests. They were to speak in such a way that unbelievers would be impressed (1 Cor. 14:24-25). The other thing is to offer real care. I've heard about soccer clubs setting up all kinds of social activities and programs for their fans: crèches, school support services, family care, hobby clubs, employment programs et cetera. These sports clubs have a better understanding of how to reach people than many a church.

2. Offer a 'want,' be a real blessing.

Building 33 really is a place of blessing for the young folks who visit. During the winter, they don't have to hang around on the streets. In the summertime, they meet here before going to other places. It's their hangout. They know they can drop in for free tea on Thursday and Friday afternoons after school if their parents aren't home. In the evenings, it offers them a place to get together and talk, or just hang out. More groups are being blessed by this place now. The church services in the pub are also a real blessing to those attending: they can give expression to their faith there without worrying about what people might think.

On Queen's Day I set up a stall on the traditional free market, offering portraits and jewelry. In my younger days, I went to an Art Academy and specialized in portraits. My daughter made beautiful jewelry and we found three guys who were willing to stand by for doing odd jobs for anyone in need of help. I made some large signs that said: Free Portraits & Jewelry. Passersby were amazed when they read those words: 'Is that stuff really free? Where's the catch?' As soon as they realized the offer was really free of charge, they thought about themselves. I guess that's what people are like. But our idea was that people would ask us to make a portrait or jewelry piece for someone else. It's a gospel principle: you receive things for the purpose of giving. So anyone who wanted to surprise someone else could ask us for a portrait, a jewelry piece or help with an odd job. It's a great way of connecting with people. Invariably, we get to share our motives, too: we do it because Jesus gave us everything He could in order for us to pass it on.

When I pastored a church, we organized neighborhood parties at one point. It's a way of showing you care about other people. The folks attending these parties really enjoyed getting to know each other in this way. For us, there was a broader context. We wanted to be a blessing to our neighborhood. We wanted to be sensitive. We wanted to be able to send a card or respond in some way if a baby was born in our area, or if someone passed away. At Christmas, we always went door to door giving people plants, along with a letter containing our Christmas wishes for them. The idea was to start doing odd jobs for people, too, but sadly there was not enough support for this within the congregation. So a lot of the campaigns we launched were partially successful. But the underlying idea was that showing kindness to our neighbors would help us develop a positive reputation in our small town, in which gossip spreads faster than light.

There are countless ways of being a blessing. Carolien travelled to the Ukraine in 2011. She went with a team of dentists who set up a dentistry inside the local church. The town in which this took place had virtually no dental facilities.

People came flocking to the church for the blessings it offered. It was a great opportunity for sharing Jesus. You could adopt an apartment building and start doing things there to bless the tenants. You could paint clowns on an old caravan and head into a deprived part of your city offering a kids' program, while also looking for other problems you might be able to fix.

If I belonged to a church with a couple of beauticians among its members, I'd sure know what to do! Today's body culture - and the distress it causes many people - offers immense opportunities for the church. You could offer the blessing of a beauty treatment, while also engaging in conversations with clients about the inner beauty that shines through when you have peace with God. Add a couple of fashion advisors, and you'd have a perfect concept. I promise you, you'll encounter a lot of frustration about physical issues. You'll need a robust counseling team. Marriage issues are also likely to spill out. A lot of marriages fail because of partners struggling with their physique. Set all of this up within the framework of your local church, and you will be exhibiting a fresh, pure gospel without having to water down the message in any way at all. What talents do your church members have? Use them to bless your neighborhood, or maybe the local refugee center or a community of immigrants in your area.

I'm still praying for COTS that we will find an opportunity to offer daytime activities or occupational therapy without placing too many demands on participants. I'd like it to be a place for people who would otherwise spend their days in emptiness and without purpose. These people are easy prey for all kinds of addictions. Offering them a place to go and engage in different activities might help them find new purpose. For example, they could make things we could then offer to people living in a home for senior citizens, or for the disabled. Other groups of people you could target with interesting activities are artists, filmmakers, dancers or journalists.

Again, there are so many ways of blessing others. Your church could organize sports and games events for the neighborhood. On the side, you could offer a Bible course or an Alpha course to those interested. If you have a few hairdressers in your congregation, you could head into a poor part of town and offer free haircuts. It would work, for sure! Or maybe your church has a couple of good amateur photographers: you could offer free portraits of children or pets. All of these ideas are ways of meeting people on their own ground and establishing contact. What about a neighborhood newspaper? Adopt a couple of streets and create a newspaper just for that area. You could do interviews to hunt for news, add some fun photos or a cartoon and put it all in a simple newspaper format for distributing door to door. Sounds like a lot of fun to me! Using advertisements, you could set up a supply and demand system connecting church members and folks in the neighborhood. For example: Babysitter looking for a job. Or: Who has a bike I can use? Or: Something need fixing? Call me. In this way, your church could present itself to the neighborhood. The contacts would follow naturally as you go about being a blessing. And you can be sure some folks will start to show an interest in your faith.

3. Be welcoming and make sure your venue is inviting.

People tend to be pretty insecure. Offer them a choice between a full restaurant bustling with activity and an empty one, and they'll chose the full one. Especially if they feel really welcome there, or if they know they'll meet friends there.

I know a person who had an ice-cream cart. Just down the road from him there was another ice-cream vendor. To lure customers away from this competitor, he told some of his customers he'd give them a discount if they stood around his cart for a while eating their ice-cream. People passing by would see all those people standing around and stop, assuming the ice-cream there must be really great.

Some churches serve coffee after the service. Unfortunately, it is usually done inside. This means no one outside the church has any idea how much people inside the church building are enjoying themselves. Church members have no way of knowing if an acquaintance of theirs happens to walk by outside - let alone inviting them in for a coffee. There has to be a better way of doing this. What if churches were to put tables and chairs outside for those who have attended the service to step out into the sun with their coffee? Everyone will see them and passersby could be offered coffee, too.

Sometimes I attend church services with a tiny group of people huddled together in a huge hall. The vast emptiness of the place almost cries out to visitors, 'This meeting is so boring, that's why there's hardly anyone here.' If you have a small group, get together in a small, cozy setting, so newcomers will have the feeling things are right. Make sure you have enough hosts and hostesses - people with a gift of recognizing hesitant or insecure people and making them feel at ease. An effective seeker service is all about striking the right note to draw visitors and newcomers into the community. A friendly welcome will make people remember a church, even if the preaching is poor. On the other hand, hearing a great sermon but being treated indifferently in a church will make a visitor think twice about ever coming back. Friendliness breaks down barriers and paves the way for relationships. The question as to whether visitors feel welcome and accepted just as they are is the most important one any community can ask itself, especially a fellowship of Christ.

4. Familiar faces!

Seeing familiar faces is also very important. It helps people overcome their hesitation. We have a large pub here in Sliedrecht that has an even larger room for shooting pool and playing darts. The guy who runs the place is always there to shake hands with almost every guest who walks through the door. The vastness of the place is compensated for by his friendliness. Take note: the most important person in the business is there to let his guests know he cares about them. If that doesn't make people feel welcome, what will?

We have an indispensable group of regular hosts and hostesses that support all our COTS campaigns. These are people who are good at connecting with newcomers, but not only that - they are also faithful. Their faithful attendance helps visitors feel at home, even if there's no one else around whom they know. They're also equipped to help people having problems.

5. Get personally acquainted with visitors.

Knowing people's names as well as certain personal details is essential in street work. I always write down the names of people I've talked to in a bar or pub, and if I think they may need follow-up, I ask for their phone number, too. I used to have business cards with my own phone number, but people will not easily call you themselves. Asking them for their number means I can call them whenever I want to.

I also try hard to remember names and facts. It's no easy feat if you're visiting bars and pubs and having two to four meaningful encounters every week. Taking notes is vital. Sometimes I will invite a person to meet up with me again for a more personal talk. We may have some French fries together; food always has a positive effect; it shows a person he or she matters to you. Another important thing is to try and be aware of special events, like birthdays or exams.

6. Go visit their hangouts and they'll dare to visit yours.

Visit the soccer club or tennis club of young people you meet. I once went and watched a guy boxing at a gym, and there's another fellow I often look up when he and his friends are making music with their band. To my surprise, the other band members are really opening up to me.

7. Think in groups.

Most people will find it easier to attend a group event if they can come with a friend. What makes it even easier for them is to hear the names of folks they've known for a long time.

8. Find ways for them to keep coming and to connect with a Christian community.

If you have an activity that attracts a certain set of people, say, an art course or a course on flower arranging, encourage participants to connect with other participants already engaged in some form of Bible study.

I hope this list of suggestions will help you set up some form of Church on the Street where you live. We've made some great discoveries so far in Sliedrecht, and new possibilities are slowly emerging all the time. You may be wondering where we get the workers needed for all these activities. Let's look at that question in the next chapter.

15. How do you find the workers you need?

By dividing the work effectively

'Then saith he unto his disciples, The harvest truly [is] plenteous, but the labourers [are] few; Pray ye therefore the Lord of the harvest, that he will send forth labourers into his harvest' (Matt. 9:37-38). Three things stand out here:

1. There is a large harvest to be had.
2. There are not many workers.
3. Prayer can move the Lord of the harvest to send out more workers.

This means that regardless of everything else it is possible to get more workers. And if there are more workers, the work of bringing in the harvest will be carried out more effectively. And then, perhaps, we will see how large the harvest really is.

These words of Matthew are very well-known. Jesus spoke them in a specific situation. I am not absolutely sure we can take them and simply project them into any and every situation related to harvesting. I do see that in my country we could be harvesting far more than we are currently doing. Some things are not going well in our work of harvesting. That's why I would like to suggest here that we need to relearn what harvesting is all about and how to do it in a new way.

First, I'd like to say something about the harvest itself in this chapter. Then I'd like to consider how we are to view the workers. I'm convinced change is needed in that area. It starts with a different perspective on the work. As we learn to see the work and the workers in a different light, we will see far more possibilities. It is quite possible that God sees far more workers than we do, simply because our perspective is wrong. In this chapter, we will discover that many different kinds of workers are needed. It all depends on where a person can be put to work and on effective division of labor. Each part of the job takes a different kind of worker who fits into that specific slot. Let us pray that God's Spirit will breathe new life into this work in our day.

That which belongs to the Lord

First, let's consider the harvest. What is it we are to harvest? We are to harvest that which belongs to the Lord of the harvest. That is what we are to bring in. That's what church is about: *kuriake*, which means, that which belongs to the *kurios*, the Lord. This may be a little confusing, but I'd like to remind you of another image of bringing in. I'm referring to the Shepherd bringing in His sheep. In this chapter, we will use both the image of the Lord of the harvest sending out workers and that of the Shepherd bringing in the sheep. Both images center on bringing together what belongs to the Lord. We often refer to street work as a form of pastoral work - a reference to the Pastor, or Shepherd. I'd like us to consider this concept a little further, as it is crucial to our work.

The pastoral road

Pastor is the Latin word for shepherd. What does a pastor do? He takes care of the flock - in this case, the flock of Jesus. One of the special things about the flock of Jesus is that we only discover where it is as we move forward in our pastoral work. Similarly, it is a gradual process: discovering what the flock needs from the Shepherd's Spirit and who on our pastoral team is best equipped to provide for that need. This is our first hint at finding workers. I believe every person who receives the Holy Spirit receives the Spirit of the Pastor, simply because the Holy Spirit is the Spirit of Christ. And He is the true Pastor. This means that every follower of the Shepherd is in some way involved in shepherding. I offer pastoral care, but I also receive it from other followers of the

Lord. I'm very much aware of this. I learn from Carolien, because she is a sincere believer who in some ways is far more like the Shepherd than I am. And there are other people in my immediate surroundings whom I learn from - people who have received the Spirit of the Pastor and, therefore, are a blessing to me. In my view, pastoral work resembles a road, a journey. The journey may begin with street work: going out onto the streets to look for sheep. A little further down the pastoral road comes the work of equipping and encouraging. And at the end of the pastoral road, a person is sent out as a worker. In this stage, people are prepared to go out onto the streets themselves. They are trained in doing street work. This view has certain implications for the task of finding workers. Giving center stage to the image of pastoral care changes everything. We discover that our understanding of finding workers has been all wrong.

The image of harvesting has led us to focus exclusively on evangelism, so we have been searching for evangelists. If that is the focus, you won't find many workers! But as we begin to see the harvest as a part of pastoral work, things change. We all have the Spirit of the Pastor living within us. You'll find this again and again as you meet other children of God. The implication is that in this Spirit we can all get involved as shepherds in bringing in the flock - each person in his or her own special position. Look at things this way and you'll suddenly find yourself seeing far more workers!

We'll think about this some more further on. But first let me share something about harvesting, or bringing in the sheep.

The Spirit singles out the sheep

We must remember that we have a very creative Shepherd. He can call His sheep from anywhere. He searches among people from all kinds of different backgrounds. He works all over the world and in many different cultures. He has innumerable keys for opening the doors to people's hearts. If He is so creative, we, too, must be creative in seeking out His sheep. At the same time, we must always be open to surprises. Our vision of the work of the Shepherd is often all too limited. Sometimes we get a glimpse. Only the Spirit of Jesus can show us where the flock is.

Sometimes the flock is joined by creatures who do not belong there. They are more like wolves (Acts 20:29-30). Other times, we find sheep belonging to the flock in unexpected places. So how do we find these sheep? By going wherever people go. There, by the grace of God, we may represent the voice of the Good Shepherd. With His Spirit, He will speak through us (John 10:4), or perhaps we will spread the sweet fragrance of Christ (2 Cor. 2:15). And who knows what will happen next!

A couple of days after I had held our first church service in a pub, I visited that same pub. I found a seat next to a guy called René. He gave me a crooked look. 'What are you sitting next to me for? I know what you want! You want to convert me! Well, I'm not interested! Thanks to you and your ministry, this whole pub has changed. Everyone's talking about last Sunday's church service. My friends aren't friends anymore. Thanks a lot!' I tried to tell him I was not out to convert him. I sincerely meant it, too, as I realized there was too much resistance. If there's no opening, you have to let go. We did have a conversation, following that first exchange. He told me about some hypocritical family members who were believers. To him, their example was enough to want to stop up his ears and avoid Christians and their fancy words. And to show me he didn't actually hate me, he bought me a beer. Whenever I see him, I notice he is keeping an eye on me. I usually just nod and leave it at that. As soon as God begins a new work in this fellow's life, I'll be sure to notice. In organized churches, I've often missed that space that is needed in order to wait on the Spirit of God. You get registered as a member and the pattern is set. Pastoral work in a setting like that easily becomes forced, even harmful.

I am deeply convinced that both the organized church and the unorganized church, as I know it, must be identified by the freedom of the Spirit. The Spirit Himself determines the order and boundaries. Our job is then to recognize and establish those boundaries in structures - just as long as everything remains subservient to the freedom of the Spirit. In this setting, certain kinds of ministers will be made manifest as we know them in our churches. Quite likely, we will also see ministers come forward to serve in entirely new ways. Technicians, scientists, artists and business people can all engage in pastoral activities, using their skills to draw people to Jesus. The Pastor is at work in them!

Some people will stand up and we will recognize in them the classic categories of pastoral ministry, such as elders, deacons, prophets, teachers and leaders. But when common believers, from office workers to mothers and children, discover that they, too, carry the work of the Shepherd within them, there will be far more workers. Give the Spirit liberty to involve them. And use this force in your community. Encourage people to explore new territories in search of the work of the Shepherd. They will find sheep. They will look for ways of bringing those sheep into Christ's fold somehow. At COTS, people soon began taking up tasks I was not getting around to. Of course, it is important that they, too, stay tuned to the Spirit and the openings He gives. The point is that together we can move forward far more effectively.

I mentioned that I believe the time has come for us to discover a new way of harvesting. This means we must go to places where there is a harvest to be gained. To my surprise, one of those places turned out to be the pub. As René said, 'Thanks to you and your ministry, this whole pub has changed. Everyone's talking about last Sunday's church service. My friends aren't friends anymore. Thanks a lot.' His comment confirms that in that particular pub there is a harvest to be brought in. We've only just begun. There is a lot of work to be done yet, but evidently there is a harvest waiting.

The Spirit appoints the workers

We need to think differently about finding workers, too. There is no strict boundary between being harvested and becoming a worker. Let me put that differently: with the Spirit of Jesus living within me, I am a shepherd and a sheep all at once. Understanding this will turn our ideas about sending out workers upside down. Every follower of the Shepherd needs pastoral care and every one of us is sent out as a shepherd. After all, everyone living in this broken world is wounded in one way or another, and needs binding up. We've all had our scrapes with the one who came 'to steal, and to kill, and to destroy' (John 10:10). Some of us have experienced his destructive power intensely. Some have been deeply traumatized by the threats thrown at them by this murderer. They live in the fear of death (Heb. 2:15). They are at risk of becoming evil, unreliable and murderous themselves (John 8:44). We can counter his power by overcoming evil with good (Rom. 12:21). This is why Jesus sent out His disciples to share blessings. It is our calling; we were meant to live lives of blessing (1 Peter 3:9). But at the same time, we need to receive blessings and encouragement from one another. In other words: pastoral care.

I received pastoral care from Co. He's that fellow I spent time with watching and discussing movies about the Bible over in his ice-cold apartment during the winter. Co's faith was still in its infancy at the time. Once I was hurrying over to his place after a church service. I was running late for our appointment, but there was another reason I was in a hurry: I was inwardly sad and restless. Certain things that had been said in the service had touched me deeply. Unexpectedly, a genuine appreciation for our work had been expressed, while for a long time I had felt as though my labor was in vain. When I arrived at Co's place, I flopped into the sofa. I was in such emotional turmoil, it seemed impossible to start watching a movie. I decided to tell Co.

'Co, you need to help me! You're my friend, right? I need you to pray for me!'

'I can't do that! I've never prayed out loud for anyone in my life.'

I told him what had happened in church. Co understood. Then I suggested that I pray first, asking God to help Co pray for me. And that's exactly how it happened. Co prayed, too. We sat there on his sofa, crying together. At that particular time, the Shepherd couldn't have chosen a better person through whom to provide me with pastoral care.

As you take your first steps on the pastoral journey you can encounter people with severe traumas, and it can be quite confusing. Sometimes people get into all kinds of trouble without realizing how close they are to destroying their own lives.

Not long ago I spoke to a 23-year-old fellow. He spent several hours crying in my arms at a bar. He had been living with a girl his age. She'd had three abortions and was now pregnant with a baby she wanted to keep. Now she had left him, taking with her everything he owned. Three years earlier, this young man had watched his mother die. She had drunk herself to death. His father by then had a new girlfriend, but she couldn't stand the boy. His father was always criticizing him, too. He had given me his phone number, so the next day I called him. He was feeling a little better. I am now looking for ways to follow up this contact. Waiting to see whether God will provide an opening. You hear a lot of stories like this one in bars. It's part of the pastoral job.

In pastoral work, your goal is to find ways in which people can make themselves useful in the Kingdom. If you recognize a desire for this in them, you equip them for certain tasks and you encourage them to press on. We're all meant to be shepherds, or pastors, serving the Lord in bringing in His flock. Anybody who is not engaged in bringing in His sheep, is scattering them. That's how forcefully Jesus put it. And He wasn't speaking to some special group of evangelists; He was addressing everyone who was there to hear (Matt. 12:30).

So how are we to look at this gathering in, or harvesting? As our understanding of this work becomes clearer, we begin to see that different workers have different tasks. Paul said one person plants, while another waters (1 Cor. 3:6-9).

The business of harvesting involves different tasks, for which different kinds of workers are needed. Some must sow or plant, others must water or protect the fields, others still must mow, bind up the sheaves, load them onto wagons, take them to the threshing floor, thresh and winnow the sheaves, separate the wheat from the chaff, store the grain in barns, and use it to make food for the master of the harvest, who supervises all the work. All of this is part of the work of harvesting. As it is a whole sequence of activities, I like to think of it as a pastoral (or harvest) line. Pastoral work begins with evangelism, but without follow-up, it will be fruitless. Each person has his or her own gift, personality and place along the pastoral road.

Only as we cover the entire pastoral road together, will there be a powerful gathering. As we recognize the need for people who can take up all those different tasks, we begin to discover that the Lord of the harvest wants to deploy far more workers than we ever imagined. As the Spirit begins to work, we will see the workers increasingly understanding where the Lord wants to position them in the whole process. They may find themselves a lot closer to the beginning of the pastoral road than they had ever thought they would be. Before we end this chapter, I'd like to list some of the possible tasks in harvesting, as a further incentive to identifying more workers.

Some possible tasks in harvesting

1. The contacter

Contacters sow or plant and are supported by those who give water. In our monthly church services at the pub, we need workers who can make visitors feel at home. Their enthusiasm helps people feel comfortable. A seed just beginning to grow is watered by these people: they get the feeling their presence in the service really matters. These contacters are indispensable, especially the ones who give water! A contacter may never consider him- or herself an evangelist, but his or her work is of immense importance to the harvest. Contacters can also be folks who take care of all kinds of odd jobs or get involved in practical ministry, so that Christians are perceived as a real blessing. Again, many of these workers have no idea of how vital their role is in the harvest.

2. The gatherers

These are workers with a focus on bringing in the harvest. They are always looking for possibilities to bring other people along to group meetings, or to deepen contacts, for example, by visiting people. Their aim is to put people in contact with others, so that they can go to a group together. They send cards to new contacts, or drop in on birthdays to give a present. I know some workers who are incredibly creative in this area. Their work is so important!

3. The caregivers and keepers

These workers see to it that the harvest is made ready and the grain can be put to use. They like to encourage others to grow. They look for growth barriers and contribute to their removal. They look for the gifts in others and for ways of preparing those others for putting their gifts to good use. The more these workers see how they are contributing to preparing people for being sent out into the harvest, the more effective their work becomes.

4. The senders

These workers have an antenna for possibilities of gathering in a harvest in new places. They bless people who, they feel, are gifted for that particular work. They send people out on missions and inspire those they've sent out. The better they are at their job, the greater the harvest.

5. The watchers

These are workers who monitor the whole process, making sure things are running smoothly and no one is at risk of getting stuck or losing the way. They are good at encouraging co-workers and offering new perspectives. They know when things need straightening out or when it's time for a totally new approach. These are probably the 'elders' mentioned in the Bible. It is not easy to say in detail what the work of elders in the Bible involved, but what seems to be clear is that their job description did involve some of the tasks of a watcher.

All of these workers need each other. Only as they move forward together, will they form a powerful team. Then we can prayerfully anticipate a growing harvest.

Part of gathering in the harvest is separating the wheat from the chaff. This separation process is usually thought to refer to the distinction between people who are followers of Jesus and those who are not. But the separation of wheat and chaff must also take place within our own hearts. So you may notice that some people are not really followers of Jesus, but you may also find they are just not ready yet: the process of separating the wheat from the chaff is still taking place within them. Jesus spoke of this when He used the image of pruning, or purging, fruit branches (John 15:2). Someone who has never before been a worker in the harvest must learn how to become one. The Holy Spirit must separate the wheat from the chaff in his personal life. In the next chapter, we'll discuss some of the challenges involved in this transition.

16. How does someone who was not a worker before become one?

A glimpse into the change processes of Alie, Henk and Merel

When a person begins to believe that God sent Jesus to this earth to be his Savior, that's a great start. But believing is not everything. Demons believe, too, 'and tremble' (James 2:19). What is needed is conversion. Conversion always consists of several phases. The first phase is that your conscience begins to bother you (Rom. 2:15; Acts 2:37). You know you need salvation. The next phase is that you find you are secure in God's love, because of the work of Christ. You're safe in His hands (John 10:27-29), He has paid for your sins (Acts 2:38). Then follows another vital phase - one that is often neglected by believers: the phase of bearing fruit (John 15:8; Acts 2:47). That is where the Spirit wants us to be. Bearing fruit, basically, is receiving His work in your life. Along with it, you experience love, joy, peace and all those beautiful attributes of God in your life (Gal. 5:22). There are other ways of saying this, too. As for me, I like to compare this change process with heading out to sea on a sailboat.

Allow the Spirit to put wind in your sails

Conversion means you no longer hoist your sails to catch the wind of all kinds of worldly spirits; instead, you deliberately opt for the wind of God's Spirit. You seek to catch it, so that you will be driven in the direction He wants you to go. Often, you will see the sails flapping about wildly in different kinds of directions. At one moment the wind of the Spirit prevails, at another the winds of the world seem to be stronger. But real, inward conversion involves a deliberate decision of the will to be led by the Spirit. It is the surrender of one person to Another. This is what God longs to see.

This decision will determine how God judges you, not your success or your decent lifestyle.

Our success in leading a decent life is often pretty disappointing anyway (Rom. 7:14-17). God's salvation is for people who have had enough of the misery of being driven along in the wrong direction (Rom. 7:24-25). You could say there are three separate steps to take:

1. Faith - based on knowing where the wind of salvation is blowing from.
2. Conversion - you hoist your sails to catch that wind, applying your seeking will to set course towards a life of grace.
3. Following - the wind of the Spirit blows you towards the likeness of Jesus, steadily causing your actions to become His.

These are the big steps. But in real life we usually take many smaller steps along the way. Sometimes we see people backsliding, too, or backing away from steps they've taken.

A changed artist

Imagine this: an artist comes to faith. From now on, he really wants to live the life of a follower. All kinds of things start changing in his life. Old habits fade away and new ones take their place. But what about his natural artistic gift? Presumably, he will carry on making the same kind of paintings for a while. But something new will emerge, too. He will learn to ask for a blessing over his work before he starts, and when a painting is finished, he will thank God for it. Then a second step will follow. He will begin to ask himself whether he should change his themes, or aspects of them. Yet another step further, he will try to figure out how to use his art for blessing other people. All of this is a growth process. He will learn to baptize his gift, that is, to cleanse it of all that does not belong to Jesus and to allow the Spirit to fan it into flame, so that increasingly he will center on serving Christ through his work. If this artist goes further still, he will develop a desire to live a purer life for God and every part of his life will be so ablaze with the Spirit that he will become a more and more effective instrument in God's hand. He will find himself praying for his commissioners and about what he might make for them. He will be so full of the Spirit that those whom he works for will be deeply touched. His paintings will take on prophetic meaning, giving voice to the Word of God and its life-changing power. I have seen this happen at our discipleship school. A participant prayerfully made a painting for another participant. The receiver saw her own life reflected and was profoundly comforted.

A process of rebirth

Unfortunately, the road from faith to conversion and on to the following of Jesus is strewn with traps and pitfalls. It cannot be charted. In the cases of Henk, Alie and Merel, things turned out very differently from what I had imagined. It was as if God wanted to show me that I cannot predict the path of the wind and shouldn't even try. God's planning is not my planning (Is. 55:8). I had to unlearn every kind of attempt to push things through - a lesson God has had to teach me before, I'm afraid. Rebirth is, and always will be, a miracle.

At the spiritual birth of a person, powerful forces are at play - forces beyond the control of human pastoral abilities. Only God can cause a heart to be born again. As His children, we may watch and wait patiently in order to connect with whatever God is doing in the new life being brought forth.

See the figure on the next page.

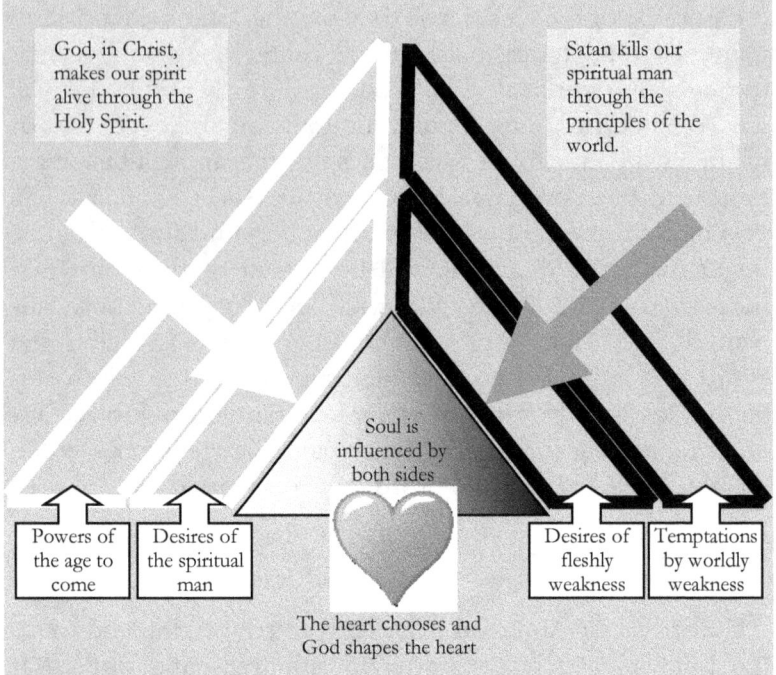

Like a natural birth, a rebirth is accompanied by all kinds of things we cannot control. In the case of a natural birth, the forces of life come into action from the inside out. The invisible life matures and when it is ready, these forces cause it to come out. The baby is separated from its former existence within the mother's womb, and the pressure pushing it towards its new life increases until it is strong enough for the baby to appear as a new being. All a mother does, when the time is right, is to cooperate with the movement she feels in her own body. She has to be careful not to force anything and when she does begin to apply her strength, she has to keep in step with the dance of the labor pains. She has no control over the pace of this dance.

It is the same when a person is born again. All a spiritual obstetrician can do is to offer a little nudge here and there when he sees God is doing something. If you start giving instructions at the wrong moment, you will counteract the rebirth and hinder the Spirit who is bringing forth this new life. You have to know how to wait (compare John 16:12-15). The miracle of new life comes from the eternal Life Giver Himself. You will see wrong connections belonging to the old life come undone. You will sense this incomprehensible urging of the Spirit and, sure enough, a new, true life will begin to unfold before your eyes.

Sometimes things can happen pretty quickly. Often the process consists of many small steps. Sometimes the labor pains start up and then stop for a while. As a spiritual obstetrician, you need to develop a feeling for this. You must be careful not to rush things, while making sure you offer new points of connection when they are needed. As soon as the new will of a born again person begins to speak out clearly, indicating what it wants and what it does not want (Rom. 7:16-18), you will know the new life has broken through. This person has been delivered from the old life (Rom. 7:24-26). The sins he now commits are not part of his new life; they are merely the afterpains of the former life that is passing away with a few last pangs.

Henk

He came along with his girlfriend. She is a Christian, but she had her doubts about the genuineness of Henk's faith. He said he believed, but she saw him doing things that were not compatible with a life of faith. His faith was immature and vague. In the past, he had messed around in relationships and with drinking. He was not yet free of all that. A spiritual obstetrician urging him to start pushing would have caused damage. His girlfriend wanted to push. She wanted Henk to change right away! He was a believer, wasn't he? Yet he still got drunk, and pretty often, too. And he couldn't keep away from slot machines either. No wonder. This guy had practically grown up in a bar. A few short prayers will not change an entire way of life. While the old life was still at work within him, something else was also stirring in Henk. He felt inwardly drawn to the invisible. He forefelt things. He knew there was more to reality than meets the eye. It was not difficult to talk to him about spirits. He was aware of their existence. And everything that happened to him in this area had a profound impact on him. When I prayed for him for the first time, a shiver passed through his body and he was covered in goose bumps. Henk had an antenna for these things. It turned out he had needed that antenna, as his father had been an unreliable, coldhearted man. In order to anticipate his father's outbursts of evil, Henk had developed a special sensitivity. He sensed the spiritual world at work in his father's soul and was subconsciously aware of the influence of this spirit on the family in which he lived. God used that antenna to warn Henk. Henk did not know this, of course. But his antenna was always switched on - and the chance of it connecting him with evil forces was significant. His inquisitive nature meant he was open to everything. That explains why his girlfriend had no trouble at all in getting him to come along to a Bible study at Building 33. He was interested.

Alie

Alie was a woman who had actually become entangled in some wrong connections. Longing for the warmth of an authentic, inner sense of connection, she started visiting fortune tellers and paranormal fairs. A form of syncretism began to grow within her. She sought high and low, hoping to find connections that would fill the emptiness inside. By the time we met, she felt the presence of spirits everywhere. She was no longer alone - but the presence of spirits from the past frightened and paralyzed her. Her loneliness and isolation deepened. This longing for connection had begun at her birth, which had been problematic. As she grew up, she felt closed in by a wall of fear and coldness. Her parents were mistrustful, broken people. They were the ones who raised the emotional wall Alie was aware of. Her mother had spent time in a Japanese camp during World War II. Her father, an only child, had been raised by a manic-depressive mother. The years of tension, insecurity and even the threat of death had left their mark on these two parents. To make matters worse, Alie had been raped as a young girl by a man she knew by name. Later, she married a traveling man who had lovers all over the world. Of course, he wanted to have sex with her, too, when they were together. But her body had gone numb. Every time they had sex, she felt her body turn into a chunk of flesh without any feeling. He told her she was crazy and humiliated her. Once he hit her so badly her nose went crooked. Their marriage didn't last. When he died, she found the inner space to begin a new search.

When I got to know Alie, the Holy Spirit was already causing some major changes in her life. A short while before, she had been baptized, but she had not yet found a community in which she could live and grow as a child of God. She had a desperate longing for delivery. She told me the entire right side of her body was numb. It was the side on which her husband had beaten her. Several of her physical functions were off whack. She was still haunted by voices and strange beings. She felt like she was floating in the air and could fall to the ground at any moment. She carried herself in a cramped, upright position, for fear of falling to the right. Every time I prayed with her, she felt a little stronger and some of the feeling in her body returned. I saw great potential in our contact. Only later did I realize I had been in too much of a hurry.

While praying for Henk and Alie, I felt this strong urge to involve them in our discipleship school. That June, we were going to end the program with a module on prayerful listening[11] and prophecy. Before then, I wanted to give Henk

---

[11] This publisher does *not* advocate contemplative prayer.

and Alie some teaching on these topics. My plan was to rope them in for the discipleship school to see how the Holy Spirit would work through these two individuals. I was certain they would experience new connections, and in my mind's eye I saw wonderful things happening in the lives of Henk and Alie. They were both so sensitive to what was going on in the spiritual world. All they needed was to be cleansed and they would be wide open to the voice of the Holy Spirit. With their consent, I had prayed for delivery from bondage to evil spirits for both of them. They were ready for this, I was certain, and they were eager to get familiar with the practice of prayerfully listening to God's voice, as we taught it in our discipleship school. Unfortunately, I was wrong.

That April, Alie suffered a terrible panic attack. She had some problems in an area of her life she had kept hidden from me. Now her troubles were mounting. She ended up in a psychiatric hospital. Initially, it was suggested she would need a year to recover. My plan was ruined. It wasn't restored either, although, thankfully, I didn't have to wait a year to get back to work with Alie. Unexpectedly, after seven weeks of sleep treatment she was doing a lot better.

When we met again, she looked different. She was still frail and unable to attend meetings at Building 33. I assumed I would have to wait patiently. But just a couple of weeks later, she called.

'Come over quickly! So much has been happening. I feel I could dance. It's amazing!'

I went over as quickly as I could. When I saw her, I was struck by the change in her posture and movement. Before her hospitalization, she would stand there looking like a gray board and when she sat down she looked as dull and lifeless as a statue. Her face, back then, had been like a piece of moving plastic. Now, it was radiant. She stood there swaying like a model in a perfect pose. Then she sat down cross-legged on her sofa and ran her fingers through her hair like some movie star. I couldn't believe my eyes. Could a person really change that much? Was this real? Was some strange supernatural force at play here? What was it? Alie began to explain.

'God has worked a miracle. I have peace now with my parents and with my ex. I'm getting answers to so many questions. They're all around me, but I'm no longer afraid, all is well. I'm getting answers by reading the Bible, watching TV and through random things I see and hear. There's wisdom in all religions.'

That scared me. There were spirits all around her? And what about all those religions?

Persistent afterpains

She sensed my hesitancy and asked whether she'd done something that wasn't right. I knew that when Alie said something, you usually had to think about her words a little longer than you do when other people say something. She says things in a way of her own - and it seemed so now more than ever. She spoke of her grandmother, who had planted the seeds of a strict Christian faith in her young life - a solemn kind of Christianity, even slightly oppressive. Women in her church were not allowed to attend services with uncovered heads. But Alie had broken free from all that. As she put it herself: 'The die is cast, the hat has passed!' She laughed out loud.

It was easy to understand her laughter. I pictured a church with dice rolling and black hats falling. It was Alie's way of describing spiritual renewal. At one point, she jumped up to pick up a safety pin - one of those cotton diaper attributes. Holding it triumphantly in the air as if it were a waving banner, she exclaimed: 'This is it! Sperm cell, ovum, conception and... new life!' I guess that's one way of putting it. It was her creative way of communicating. Yet she did keep using words and terms I had difficulty interpreting. She started talking about her belief in reincarnation. When I responded by saying that reincarnation is a central tenet of Hinduism, she immediately backed away from it: 'No, I don't believe that. New life, that's what I believe in!'

I talked some more about Buddhism and how its view on human suffering is so radically different from Christ's teachings. She unequivocally sided with Christ. All the differences in religions had nearly driven her crazy in the past, but now she could handle this whole area calmly. I asked her about her old contacts, worried that she might have come under the influence of the spirits of deceased people.[12]

'No, no, it's not that, it's just I feel I've finally been able to process everything that happened in the past. Now the memories of it all can float around me without scaring me. Now I can put that Indonesian painting my mother gave me back on the wall in my room...' Her eyes were shining, as if to say, 'Listen carefully now!' Then she continued. 'I had a dream about Building 33. I saw it right before my eyes. I know I belong there. I can't come just yet, because I have to regain my strength first. I'm better at setting my own boundaries now, too. But I feel so much stronger than ever before. I'm going to come over. Just what I'm going to do there, I'm not sure - but I'm coming!' When I left her place, I was overflowing with joy - but I also felt very small. That's how God works. He doesn't need little Mr. Vrooland and all his plans and good intentions. I was sure now that everything was going to work out for Alie. But alas - a psychosis followed. And looking back, I should have seen it coming.

When a person comes to faith, old habits and patterns don't just disappear. You have to be aware of that. His or her connection with God's guidance still has to grow.

See the figure on the next page.

---

[12] Actually evil spirits of course.

What had happened thus far? A new life had begun in Alie. But the afterpains echoing her old life were so powerful that the new life could not manifest itself very clearly yet. She has been going through very tough times, but she has kept fighting. After a long period of psychiatric treatment, she has made some recovery. I'm still looking forward to that moment when she joins one of our groups. Unfortunately, she still dreads the idea. You see, I thought she would quickly become a co-worker. But her wounds from the past were deeper than I could have imagined. For now, my job is to wait patiently. God is at work.

New disappointments

As for Henk, my plans for him also fell through. At first, things seemed to be going really well. During a one-on-one meeting, I shared with him some of the considerations involved in prayerful listening. It made him more excited than he already was about exploring this new spiritual world. He had not yet been baptized, so I asked him whether he was ready for that step. He was, he told me. So I gave him some teaching on baptism, along with another lady. The date for their baptism was set in June. Following that, I planned to introduce Henk to our discipleship school, so he could practice prayerful listening with the other participants. I really liked this orderly plan. At his baptism, we would pray for Henk to be filled with the Holy Spirit, preparing him for the experiences awaiting him in the discipleship school.

Just what happened in the invisible world, I don't know. Henk started talking to people about his upcoming baptism. And from every side, people started opposing the idea. He was especially discouraged by church people and folks who had been raised going to church. They strongly objected to the form and the place of Henk's baptism 'This can't be right!' they said. Henk began to wonder whether he really was ready for baptism after all.

There were four candidates for the baptismal service that June. Three of them met severe opposition from relatives and friends, and two of them yielded to this pressure. One of them was Henk. He showed up for an introductory lesson on prayerful listening at the discipleship school, but after that we didn't see him in class nor in the group he belonged to. He said it was because things had gotten really busy at work; he needed to slow down, he said. I started bumping into him more frequently at one of the bars than at the group meetings he had attended. He did say he wanted to stay involved at COTS. We're still hoping and waiting. God has done so much in his life, I expect the Spirit will continue to tug at his heart. But evidently there are other forces pulling at him as well. For now there is no plan for a baptism, there have been no further conversion steps, and there is no sign of Henk becoming a worker. It's in the hands of the Shepherd!

Merel

With Alie being temporarily out of the game, I was somewhat at a loss. Soon I started looking around for new openings. 'What is God doing with whom?' I began to put my hope in Merel. Why? Because she told me she often had premonitions about things. To me, this meant she had the capacity to be receptive to the Holy Spirit. She was like Henk and Alie in that respect. Apart from that, though, she was quite different. She had been baptized as an infant. Her family background was pretty typical of the sixties in the Netherlands: a no-nonsense, hard-working mentality with a focus on making a living, and little room for showing affection. Merel, on the other hand, was hungry for new experiences. As a young woman, she started experimenting with drugs, drink and kicks. I got to know her at a pub. During our conversations, she was quick to share about her new-found, somewhat shaky faith. 'I believe in my own way and I can easily get cynical about faith.' She had an ambivalent friendship with a Christian girl. Sometimes she felt sympathy, at other times she felt a loathing. This friend was trying to impose things on Merel for which she wasn't ready. Her exaggerated way of saying things annoyed Merel. Merel knew her friend was not a very balanced person, which aroused her sympathy. She was one of those people who can easily get angry at a person and then just as easily make up.

She started attending services at the pub. Our contact deepened a little. Because of her chaotic history, her unemployment and a bunch of other issues that really confused her, she struggled with depression.

It is true that with the power and the armor of God, we can resist temptation and evil influences. But making a drawing of this battle is a lot easier than actually engaging in battle!

On the other hand, she exhibited tremendous resilience and spunk. I already mentioned her ability to blow her top. It was just one expression of this lady's inner strength. Being a broken person and yet having the spirit to stand up and shake a fist at the world can easily go together. In our email exchanges, she could tear people to pieces the way a ravenous lion might use its jaws to rip up its prey. Her amazing creativity in using vivid language and neologisms often took me by surprise. Coupled as it was to a hatred that really scared me, I often asked myself, when she was busy tearing her latest victim apart, 'What on earth am I doing? Does she really mean this?' A glance at her eyes usually suggested she did. But then, if I listened a while longer, what I really discovered was a cry of the heart for genuine love and faithfulness. She was so mixed up that her purest longings found expression in the ugliest forms. I wanted so badly to share with her all the beauty of God's love, and I searched for ways to do this. Since Merel was a sensitive person, I began to hope that perhaps during the prayerful listening sessions at our discipleship school she might have some fresh experiences. When I suggested this, she was quite open to it, so I began to tell her more. We took the prayerful listening approach to pray for a friend of hers. It softened her and she began to long for more.

As the end of June neared, and the discipleship school module I wanted to involve her in was about to begin, Merel was suddenly struck by heart failure. It kept her awake for nights on end. Then more ailments were discovered. Her intention to join us at the discipleship school was undermined by a paralyzing fatigue. Another of my plans fell through. Merel felt miserable and sought comfort in a bar. Yet at the same time she had opened her mind wide to all the things I had shared with her about God. She saw what I did and longed to do things for other people herself. At this point, her creativity resurfaced. The National Zipcode Lottery here in the Netherlands had awarded a street prize to one of the

Sliedrecht neighborhoods. In the wake of the street prize came a whole string of gift tokens offering the receivers free access to Ponypark Slagharen[13], one of the Dutch theme parks.

'What a waste it is!' Merel said to me one day.

'Gerard, most of the free tickets are getting thrown away, yet there are so many young families that would be thrilled at the opportunity to go to Slagharen for a day. We should collect the free tickets not being used and offer them to families interested in using them!'

She had other great ideas and I encouraged her. 'Merel, that is so beautiful! You have such great ideas. It's God working through you!'

Merel reacted much as I might have expected: 'Those are your words. I'm not so sure!' Yet I could see in her eyes and in her whole response that being complimented in this way meant a lot to her. I believe the Spirit bound up those words in her heart. Thank you, Lord!

The local newspaper caught on to our initiative and soon everybody knew about it. Merel was in her element, doing something for other people. One day in mid-August, a busload of happy townsfolk set off for Slagharen. Merel was actively serving God and deep within her a small voice was telling her it was good. Would you call this a spectacular change? Had Merel really raised her sails to catch the wind of the Spirit? Or was this just an interesting project to her? Did it have anything to do with conversion? Was she doing the work of a harvester?

As I ponder these questions, I'm reminded of Matthew 10:42, 'And whosoever shall give to drink unto one of these little ones a cup of cold *water* only in the name of a disciple, verily I say unto you, he shall in no wise lose his reward.' And also of Matthew 25:45, 'Verily I say unto you, Inasmuch as ye have done *it* unto one of the least of these my brethren, ye have done *it* unto me.' Perhaps I try too hard to analyze and

---

[13] Pronounce with a hard 'g.'

map everything. Everything that is good, is good. Only God sees the underlying motives and movements; to Him, everything is laid bare. I'm not saying that doing good makes you a follower of Jesus. But if a desire to do good in the service of God has been planted in your heart, you have the spirit of a follower. Something within you has fundamentally changed. If you then learn to respond to this desire and to honor Him for it, you are a worker. Merel has a lot of creativity to offer in His service. Our job is to challenge and encourage her. She still likes going to bars, but she also hears that still, small voice of God. She's trying to make changes. She longs to do what is right. She hasn't grasped yet how all-encompassing God's love is, but something is moving within her. And she saw an opportunity that was neglected by many members of the organized church. This poem was written by Merel (not her real name) on July 26, 2011, at 7:14 am:

Wind

Wind, where are you going
Where will you blow
Wind, how will you get there
Who will show you the way
Wind, when do you decide
When to whisper and when to rage
Wind, can I hold you
I want to come with you

Patience, creativity and letting go

So do we now know how to turn believers into workers? No. It is another of God's great secrets. The examples of Henk, Alie and Merel offer little insight, partly because of their chaotic backgrounds. But these are the kind of people we work with. Entering into their chaotic histories, we connect with them in their search for the orderliness and direction God longs to introduce in their lives. The key lies not in our plans and ideas, but in the openings God creates in their lives. It's always a journey. As we set out, we mustn't be afraid of disappointments. The examples I've given demonstrate that we have to be alert to pick up the threads handed to us by other people, however tangled and fragile they may be. What are their interests? What goes on in their minds? How can we connect with them? At COTS we have a lady who likes to come in and clean the Building. She does it for the Lord. We must learn to appreciate her contribution as a worker. She also thrives on caring for people in Sliedrecht who have lost their way. Another lady enjoys serving coffee at our bar. She is so faithful. Because she enjoys the work at Building 33, she often invites people to attend COTS services. She sees herself as a deaconess. We're happy with that. Another woman works with the elderly. She sees them growing lonely, so she organizes COTS activities with them. She has roped in some of our young folk to walk the annual Dutch Four-Day Walk, pushing along elderly participants in wheelchairs. We could go on sharing examples like these. I chose the stories we've looked at in this chapter, because they show us it takes patience, creativity and courage to let go at times. If a person starts something new and then quits, or fails, never mind - encourage him and look for other opportunities. Watch and pray!

Exposition 3 - The binding effect of baptism: Romans 6:3-14

One way of coping with disappointment is to hold on to the deeper meaning of baptism. Baptism has a binding, uniting effect. It helps you stay connected with seekers who stumble and fall during their search.

Baptism has a binding, uniting effect

In order to benefit to the full from the binding power of baptism, we must grasp the breadth of baptism, or the work of the Spirit.

In order to catch a glimpse of the breadth of the power of baptism, let's look at how the Spirit draws people toward baptism. Paul teaches us that 'no man can say that Jesus is the Lord, but by the Holy Ghost' (1 Cor. 12:3). Where the Spirit is heard, the power of baptism is noticed. Peter recognized the work of the Spirit and couldn't wait to administer baptism (Acts 10:47). Sometimes we can see people being drawn towards baptism, even though they themselves say they're not ready for it. We may think they're being disobedient and foolish, but it is the timing of the Spirit. He reveals things to people in His own good time (Gal. 1:15-17). We must also leave the order of events up to the Spirit. Our calling is merely to connect with everything that is of God, which is revealed to us in His time.

Romans 6 gives us insight into the binding effect of baptism

Here are some lessons this passage teaches us:

1. Baptized people have been baptized into Christ's death (Rom. 6:3). Their dead works - that is, their sins and their carnal accomplishments - have been crucified. They have been rendered null and void, as far as God's Kingdom is concerned. They must not connect with the worldly spirit that causes these sinful attitudes.
2. Baptized people 'walk in newness of life' with Christ (Rom. 6:4). They have been grafted into the true vine in order to bear fruit (John 15:1-8). The works of this new life are brought forth by Christ and made visible in baptized people. We may connect with these works, this fruit, of the Spirit.
3. Unbaptized people remain subject to the power of death. Death has dominion over them (Rom. 6:9). They are dying all the time and everything they do, both good and evil, is in the process of dying with them. Their good works may have meaning for a baptized person, as all good things are intended for those who are baptized into Christ. But as far as the unbaptized person is concerned, the deeds done hang from a withered branch (John 15:6).

If you're in touch with a new convert in whom the ways of the old life are still active, you must practice viewing this person as a person baptized into Christ. It will help you stay connected and to cope with disappointments.

The life of a person not baptized into Christ is constantly in the process of dying (Rom. 6:9)

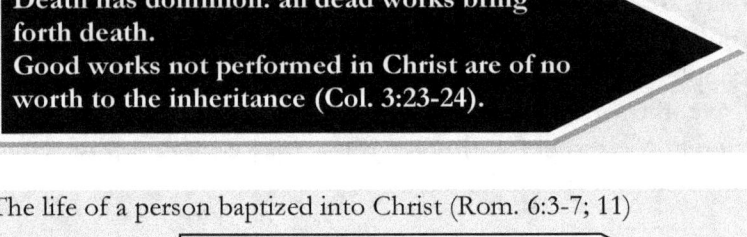

The life of a person baptized into Christ (Rom. 6:3-7; 11)

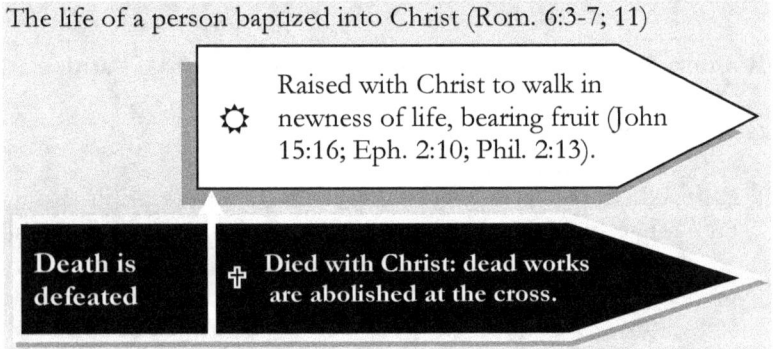

End of exposition 3 - The binding effect of baptism: Romans 6:3-14

At COTS, we call ourselves a church. We do things, as this chapter illustrates. To an outsider, our program may appear to consist of a rather strange collection of activities. At first glance, you may not associate the things we do with a church. This raises the question as to whether COTS is entitled to calling itself a 'church.' Let's look for an answer to that question in the next chapter.

17. Is it alright to call the COTS groups a 'church?'

If we can see the Lord of the harvest at work there, it's justified

I wouldn't be surprised if in Sliedrecht every bar visitor of 40 years and older knows who Sjon is. Sjon is a self-confessed alcoholic. He lost his father at a young age. Then a number of other things happened that took away his lust for life. As far as Sjon is concerned, life is not really worth living anymore. His desire is to go to God. He prays at least three times a day and God knows the cry of his heart: 'Dear Lord, please take me away.' Once, when he had made another of his attempts to arrange his own answer to prayer, his older brother Steven objected fiercely: 'I don't want to lose my brother!'

I had met Steven once before at a pub. The encounter had taken me by surprise. Sjon is so skinny and fragile, you almost want to keep praying that he won't suddenly fall apart. Steven is about four times his younger brother's size. You may want to pray he will never throw himself on top of you, because if he does, you'll be pulverized. He is this huge, square guy known all over Sliedrecht for being as strong as steel. Everyone knows Sjon is a believer. He's not ashamed of it. In fact, for a long time Sjon thought he was the only believer in his family, and others thought the same. But we were all wrong. When Steven told me about that time he got shot and that other time when his heart seemed to have stopped beating, I knew better. Steven was a believer, too. Because of my involvement with Sjon, I gradually got to know Steven. One day the three of us were having a conversation about the meaning of faith. We prayed together. Steven knew Sjon came over to Building 33 every fortnight to join one of our groups in sharing, praying and singing together. We usually watch a movie, discuss a related Bible passage and generally have a great time. 'I think I'll join you next time!' Steven said. He kept his word and started coming along with Sjon. Now he has crossed the threshold, he tells everyone the group is his 'church': 'I go to church at the Building.' That's how our center is known and I'm happy with that.

Gathering in

You might ask whether it is alright to call our center a church. I've always been pretty easygoing in my use of the word 'church' (*kuriake*). My viewpoint is simple: any group of people belonging to the Lord (*kurios*), can be considered a church. It offers a lot of room for maneuvering. In fact, things can really start to move! This movement begins the moment the Lord pours out His Spirit on people. That's when the gathering begins (Matt. 12:30). Any group calling itself the church of Christ and yet not manifesting this type of movement is falling short in an area that is vital to all God's children. The parable of the two sons, in which one of the two goes to work in the vineyard and the other doesn't, is painfully clear on this (Matt. 21:28-32). The presence of the Lord becomes noticeable the moment this movement begins! No organized church has any reason to feel safe and secure if this kind of movement is lacking. And if it does exist? Then we begin to see what I described in Chapter 15. The Spirit begins to equip workers for the harvest. Contacters, gatherers, caregivers, keepers, senders and watchers begin to rise up.

The great thing about Steven is that several times he has invited friends to come along to his church. On the other hand, he also faces resistance from some people. It comes with being a part of this movement. In groups like those belonging to COTS, this welcoming attitude towards others is quite common. It is stronger than I've ever seen it to be in any organized church. This may say something about the churches in which I've served, but I prefer to think the uncomplicated character of these groups makes it easier for participants to invite friends. In the COTS groups, you can clearly see people gathering in, whereas in the organized church you tend to see people gathering together.

Leaders in gathering in

This movement of gathering in is characteristic of the work of the Lord of the harvest. Its evident effect in our groups means we may rejoice in the presence of the Lord of the harvest. But what about the offices of the church? Do we have some kind of elder board at COTS? Encouraged by two colleagues, I have given some thought to the idea of a leadership team. But how do we tackle this at COTS? How do we align our structure with Scripture? We know that in the Bible the act of gathering in was performed under a certain oversight. The Scriptures give us the names of various offices, such as elders, overseers and deacons (Phil. 1:1), or apostles, prophets, evangelists, shepherds and teachers (Eph. 4:11). The names shed light on different gifts. The gifts observed in people are seen to be important for the work of gathering in. God wants to lead the work through people with these gifts. Officially recognizing the appointment of these people by God is a way of giving them authority on behalf of the Lord of the harvest. We can see the work of the Spirit in all of this.

So on the one hand, a church is characterized by the gathering in of the harvest, or as it is described in Ephesians, the growth of the Body (Eph. 4:16). And on the other hand, a church needs people with certain gifts to move ahead, or take the lead, in gathering in.

We formed a team of leaders at COTS. In an organized church, they would probably be called the church council, or elder board. We could call them 'elders,' but the name is of no significance to us. Neither do we want to define their tasks too rigidly in advance. They are leaders and their special gifts, combined with their love of the work, will determine their field. We don't lay down the law for them. We discuss the needs of the groups, and each individual with a specific gift is encouraged to find his or her way in helping to meet those needs. So COTS has an organizational form, but it is determined by the movement of the Spirit. If the Spirit leads us to change track tomorrow, we will. Whenever we see an organizational need, we try to respond flexibly, working with the gifts God has given us. In this way, our desire is to help every person who gathers together with us to become a worker in the harvest.

Our leadership team is made up of people who have demonstrated a clear sense of responsibility for the progress of COTS. Some of them have made substantial sacrifices to do so. The Spirit has brought to light what is in their hearts. Their examples are so pastorally grounded I am constantly learning from them what the Pastor desires to do with us. These people are a lot better at many things than I am, and they make me feel genuinely humble. I couldn't imagine a better church council or elder board for COTS than this one. And I look forward to seeing more and more gifts made manifest in this leadership team. Already, their pastoral commitment is a shining example.

Working with groups

If you're familiar with organized churches, the fact that we work with groups may seem strange to you. We don't get everyone together in a church service, in which the pastor preaches a sermon and does all the other things that come with it. I did that twice a week in the organized church and often felt very lonely standing in the pulpit. I knew I was being judged by the people in front of me. What they were thinking, I could only guess. I never knew whether my sermon was coming across or not. Sometimes a few people reacted afterwards, giving me at least some indication of what my efforts had brought about. But there were few or no heart-to-heart conversations about meeting with God and I began to miss this in our church services. Standing in the pulpit, my job was to pass on what God had taught me during my preparations. It was like chewing the cud. Sure, it was great to be together and to celebrate God's goodness with other believers. But I was never sure whether my preaching was a help or a hindrance. And I wanted to learn from them, not just teach them. I wanted to be fed by them. Isn't that how a body works? I began to miss the reciprocal encouragement. When I started working with the COTS groups, the difference became more evident than ever: mutual encouragement and sharing versus a monologue delivered from the pulpit. That's why eventually I stopped preaching in the organized church.

There doesn't appear to be much unity among our different groups. The organized church, with its streamlined Sunday services, looks a lot more unified. But we all know there are many different groups within any organized church, too. Groups in which church members share their walk with God with each other. Often, these groups are set up by the church council or elder board. They will organize Sunday school groups, youth groups, seeker services, afternoon programs for the elderly, teaching groups et cetera. So they, too, work with different groups within their congregations. At COTS, we have made a deliberate choice to focus on group work. Sometimes we all do things together and folks can get together in a larger setting. We may start working together with other churches in specific areas. We are a part of the larger Body of Christ in Sliedrecht and the worldwide Body of Christ of all times.

But groups are still our focal point at COTS. Why? Because they offer room for personal contact and heart-to-heart conversations. It is an expression of what Jesus told His disciples: if you meet someone who is open to receiving the peace of God's Kingdom, abide there (Matt. 10:11). To abide somewhere means to stick around and develop a sense of fellowship in Christ. In the early days of Christianity, home churches popped up everywhere. That's what we have in mind. I am constantly asking myself how we can form suitable groups. Identifying a group is one thing, but encouraging its members to become group people is another. Sometimes you think you've formed a great group, and then something flares up, causing the whole group to fall apart. If it were a matter of DNA, I would say a lot of folks have a greater genetic tendency to quarrel and fall out than to be loyal and stick together. To church folk, going to church is the normal thing to do. Even if there are tensions among them causing them to ignore one another, they still get together. Church attendance is a part of their weekly program. Most people do not share this habit. Many of us resist committing, or binding, ourselves to others and can come up against a wide variety of barriers. Yet at the same time, my experience has taught me that people do have a basic longing to stick with a group once they have become part of it. They have to learn that faithfulness causes group members to grow towards one another. One of the conditions is that the group size should always remain manageable - so that participants can be open and trust each other.

Faithfulness and daring to trust are the first step. But there's more. Group members must also be given responsibility. They must become workers. We must always be looking for ways in which to use the gifts of group members - in group activities as well as beyond the group. This is part of the plan of the Lord of the harvest. This may be easier to accomplish in one group than in another. But we must be open to surprises. I already mentioned the fact that we have several folks who are always inviting others to come along. These people are well on their way to becoming good workers.

How the Body works

We've already come across the image of the body. This image is used extensively in 1 Corinthians 12, where the Church is introduced as the Body of Christ.

Exposition 4 - Bound together in one Body: 1 Corinthians 12:12-27

It is amazing how in every group each individual has possibilities that others in that group do not. Every time we connect with a person who is interested in joining one of our groups, we connect with that person's friends, too. We also find that this person has something about his character that enables him to reach out to people we would never be able to reach ourselves. Teenagers attract teenagers. Alcoholics attract other alcoholics. This is one of the principles of the Body. It is how the Body of Christ is fully activated, as God binds people together using human bonds (Hos. 11:4).

Through the Spirit we are baptized into one Body (1 Cor. 12:12)

1. Differences within the Body are necessary. Different functions enable the Body to operate healthily in different tasks for which it has been placed in this world (1 Cor. 12:17).
2. These differences must be bound together, while always retaining their own uniqueness, in order to support one another in the work of the Body (1 Cor. 12:21).
3. The so-called weakest parts of the Body need extra protection, as they are of special importance to the Body (1 Cor. 12:22-24).

Paul calls us members of the Body of Christ. You could say a member is a cell - the smallest individual part of a Body. Each cell has its own task and works together with a group of cells (see Exposition 1). A cell group, then, is a larger unit within the Body. Each cell group, in turn, works together with other cell groups. Together, they make up the complexity of the larger Body of Christ.

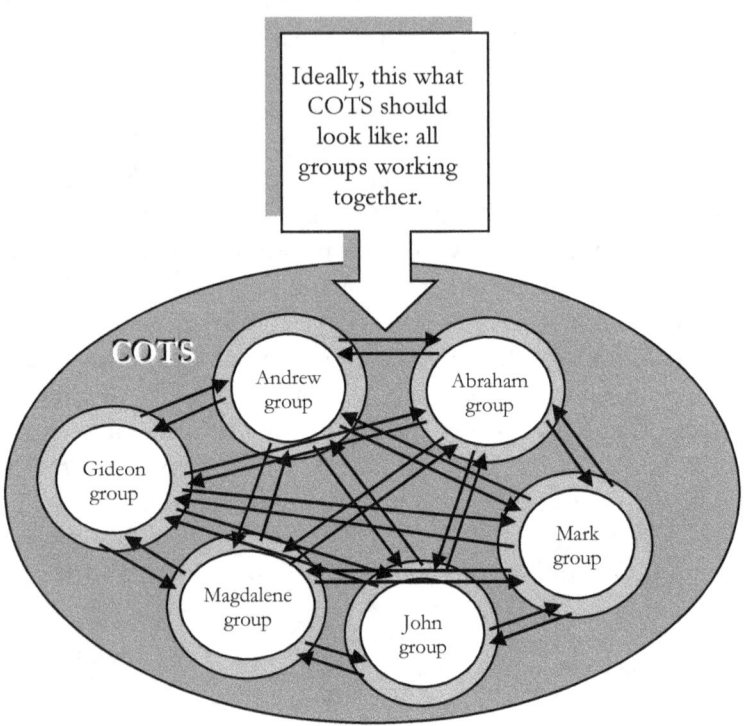

This same diagram could be used to model all the different churches in Sliedrecht, with each one reaching out to a different group of people and the whole working together for the greater good of the community. In this model, the different churches also support and encourage one another.

See the figure on the next page.

Is it alright to call the COTS groups a 'church?'

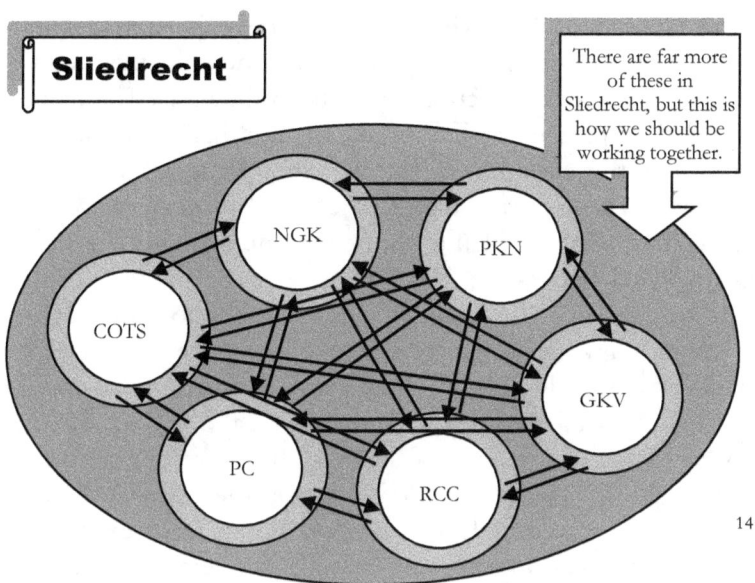

This is how the different churches in a country should work together with each other and with churches all over the world. We should recognize the work of Christ in one another, and encourage and support one another in growing towards Him. We confess that we are one in Christ, but sadly we do not experience this unity the way we are meant to. COTS has this problem, and so do many other churches all around the world. Nonetheless, we do keep placing our trust in the work of Christ (keep in mind that cooperation is only possible on the basis of the truths mentioned in Exposition 3).

End of Exposition 4 - Bound together in one Body: 1 Corinthians 12:12-27

A human body is one big system of giving and receiving. How does it work? The stomach sends off a signal saying

---

[14] NGK is the Dutch Reformed Church; PKN is the Reformed Church; GKV is the Christian Reformed Church; PC is the Pentecostal Church; RCC is the Roman Catholic Church. As mentioned above, cooperation is only possible on the basis of the truths mentioned in Exposition 3.

food is needed. The eye receives this signal from the brain and looks for information on where to find something edible. The legs receive instructions to walk to the table. The hand is signaled to pick up a slice of bread. The hand then lifts the bread to the mouth, which, in turn, passes it on to the stomach. The stomach digests the bread in order to provide all of the members of the body with energy. This is a how a normal body works.

It is also how the Body of Christ ought to work. It is a system of giving and receiving. Whenever the system fails, parts of the body die off. They cease to function or to have any meaning in the body and, therefore, the connection falls apart. On top of this, a healthy body lives for certain purposes. If there is a lack of purpose, the entire body ends up being occupied with the question why it really exists. This is where depression and suicidal behavior enter in. The Body of Christ has a very clear purpose: to gather in. This is also the challenge we now face at COTS, with all the possibilities given us and the capacities we have to overcome barriers. It will only work if the Holy Spirit breathes His life into us.

An eye is no fingernail

I discovered the importance of being a member of a body when I stopped pastoring a regular church. In my final year there, I was given several subtle hints suggesting I stop meddling with the development of the church. I was allowed to attend services and fill in my last few services according to schedule, but being a part of the process, developing vision and helping to build up the church - those tasks were no longer mine. I had become a paper member, rather than a member available for deployment. I felt like a dead part of the body. Everything within me that was geared to serving God had to be deactivated. I'm not suggesting this particular body had switched on some brutal rejection mechanism, but I was like an eye accustomed to recognizing needs but had been turned into a fingernail - a member designed to complete the body, but with minimal responsibility. I felt underrated and started looking for places where I might function the way I really am. That's one reason I was so happy when we started the discipleship school and the Sunday afternoon group. There I was able to give and to receive in a way that worked for me. I learned from this that as a member you need a body in which you can function. A place where you are wanted the way you are. If you don't have this, you slowly begin to die. You become a spectator of what that is going on in the local representation of the Body. We want to avoid that happening to anyone at COTS.

The sacraments

At COTS we want to link the use of people's individual gifts to our celebration of the sacraments. We want people to recognize that their lives are being driven forward by a new Spirit. The celebration of Communion offers us an important lesson in this area. It visibly demonstrates that Jesus wants to indwell your body, mine, and the body of the person next to us. This is very important to our members! 'You and me, along with him and her... we belong together.' The purpose is that the Life of Jesus becomes visible in those receiving Communion. The flesh and blood of Jesus in human beings! Jesus longs to manifest His power and active involvement in these people's lives. 'You and you and you must now go and do what Jesus did.' There is no condemnation, as partaking in Holy Communion involves complete forgiveness of all your sins as well as those of others participating.

Baptism teaches us a similar lesson. In baptism, Jesus washes over us, as it were, like a layer of liquid gold covering a rotten piece of wood.[15] The gold hardens. The process of

---

[15] Here the author tries to combine two realities into one picture (simul sanctus, simul peccator, or the objective position in Christ and the subjective experience on earth).

decay is stopped. There is this beautiful glow. This is how we can shine through baptism! Getting baptized won't make us as pure as He is, but more than anyone else, God will delight in our radiance. And people will notice, too. They will begin to sense that we belong to Him! His Spirit will be at work in us! So can Steven call the group he attends at Building 33 a 'church?' I think so, simply because it is a place where the Spirit of God moves in connection with God's worldwide Body of all times.

In the last section of this book, I'd like to look briefly at our expectations for the future of COTS, while sharing some of the main developments we have seen so far.

The current and future connections of COTS (Chapters 18-19)

In Chapter 18, I would like to briefly share with you our prayer for the future of COTS. In Chapter 19, we'll look back at how the COTS community officially got started.

18. What is our prayer for the future?

Longings, prayers and frailty

We've shared with you how important personal contact is in the vision that underlies COTS. God is the purest Person. He is the Person from Whom the existence of every other person flows. He works through personal contact, and He binds people together into one Body. This body lives and moves with the purpose of gathering in a harvest. He brings this about through acts of love aimed at caring for people's needs and through personal interaction. This is how He works through people. It also explains why Jesus had to become a man to demonstrate the Personhood of God here on earth.

The purpose of groups

We work with different groups at COTS in order to protect this personal contact as much as we can. We want these groups to remain manageable. Through the personal contacts fostered in these groups, the work of the Spirit is made manifest more quickly than it would be otherwise. In a group, it's easy to see how another person is doing. The spirits of this world also become more manifest in small groups. This makes group work powerful, but delicate, too. In a group, you are constantly on the alert for what is happening and how to respond. That's the big challenge: sensing what is going on in the group.

At COTS, we distinguish several phases in group development:

1. Gathering people in to be with other people with whom they feel at ease, and giving them a foretaste of God's love.
2. Nourishing these people in such a way that they begin to see themselves as a group, while also giving more space to the grace of God in their individual lives.
3. Nourishing them so that they begin to grasp the mystery of how Jesus works through His Body on this earth, recognizing that their own group can be a reflection of His Body, while also being a part of the larger worldwide Body of Christ of all times.
4. Discovering the gifts within the group, celebrating the sacraments of the Body of Jesus (baptism, anointment, communion, division of labor) and teaching on how the Body is designed to engage in the work of gathering in.
5. Connecting each group to other COTS groups through joint celebrations and, if possible, making connections with other groups in the organized church.

We have a number of different groups at COTS now, and our aim is to nourish them so that the developmental phases we just looked at become visible in them. We are in constant need of God's wisdom for discerning which steps to take.

The points listed above follow a certain order. God is a God of order, yet His order is subject to the freedom of the Spirit. Every time a person joins a group, new gifts are added - and every time someone leaves, certain gifts go with him. Every time a group member grows, or stumbles and falls, God's order is affected. It's part of the dynamic of the Body. The wellbeing of a single member influences the whole, just as the suffering of one affects all (1 Cor. 12:26). The more powerful the expression of the members' gifts, the more lively the Body dynamics.

Prayers

We have a long way to go, but our prayer at COTS is that we will experience all of this to the full, growing in unity and service.

We always try to be alert to the possibility of new groups. If a person gives me the impression he is open to discussing the Gospel in more depth, I immediately and prayerfully begin to look for a group he might participate in.

In this context, we are also praying that God will give us an opening to Sliedrecht's Islamic community. We have contacts at the mosque, and at Building 33 we've gotten to know quite a few Muslims from the street.

We also want to build bridges to organized churches and groups. If the work of COTS or Building 33 is ever forced to stop, we want our believers to be able to connect with other Christians in Sliedrecht.

Another prayer item is that we will be able to develop daytime activities and forms of occupational therapy for people who struggle to fill in their days. Boredom can cause people to end up hanging out in bars or getting hooked on other addictions, so this would be a great extension of our ministry. We would also love to see retired professionals joining us. If we could then get businesses to rope us in for odd jobs, these older folks could use their skills and experience to team up with some of our young people in need of work experience. A pool of artists and other gifted people would enable us to further broaden our range of daytime activities.

Another area in which we would like to get involved is helping people who have lost their homes. I wouldn't be surprised if the spirit of iron and clay (Dan. 2:43) gains more and more strength in our country, and more and more people will experience rejection by others. We've met numerous young people who are no longer welcome at home, because they cause too much trouble for their parents. Who else can they turn to? Others have been thrown out of their homes by people they lived with. There are many different reasons why this can happen. Sometimes we have little choice but to guide such a person to one of the Salvation Army facilities. On other occasions, we've been able to share God's love more abundantly. These situations are always a challenge. As our resources are limited, the help we can offer is usually very basic. My prayer is: 'Lord, give us the means and the faithfulness to embrace these people and to offer them a safe haven!'

Carolien and I are not exactly youngsters ourselves, so another prayer of ours is that in time people will step forward to take over from us. They must be people who genuinely care about others and are willing to sacrifice everything. Faithfulness and creativity are key. But the most important thing is that they firmly hold God's hand as humble servants of the One Who *is* love. When these new leaders step up, they will do things differently from us. There's nothing wrong with that, it's part of the dynamic of the Body.

We also pray we will be able to contribute to the work of other pioneers in God's Kingdom. We're aware of our influence, as we get a lot of questions. Each person must find his or her own place and role in the Kingdom. Copying our ministry is impossible, because we're 'we' and we do things as God enables us to do them. Other people will find other paths. Each of us must learn to listen personally to God's promptings. His creativity knows no bounds, so everything is possible. In my view, seekers in our country are crying out for this spiritual creativity and for people willing to pay the price - to surrender everything you have, so that God can use everything He has invested you with. Don't panic if you spend months in tears. Sometimes, that's what it takes; it is the pain of new creativity. Artists often experience long periods of restlessness in the run-up to new breakthroughs. Sometimes people who are about to be used by God spend weeks and months crying. If this happens to you, it is the restlessness of God moving within you. He is preparing you for new things in His great work of art. That's how we got involved in the COTS community. Through sorrow. One step at a time. It was like a long series of callings.

19. The COTS fellowship

A series of callings

When do you know you have a calling to plant a church? Generally speaking, that is a tough question to answer. A calling is not something you can organize. A wise person once told me the place to look for your calling is where your passion meets an external need. Of course, that's assuming both the passion and the need are in accordance with the will of God. After all, there are godless, even demonic passions and needs, too. But if you your passion meets a need and both coincide with God's will, you have a basic starting point.

That's how I began. It started with an inner urge. I arrived in Sliedrecht in 1999 and as I cycled through the city, I saw its people and felt a strong inner conviction that I was to be a pastor to those people. Why? It didn't seem to make much sense. But I was already being drawn to the streets of Sliedrecht. Of course, I was light-years away from founding a Church on the Street. It was a long process of growing towards that point. Like a series of small callings gradually taking my life in a certain direction.

Luuk and Tom

Luuk was part of the process, too. I had had my eye on him for several years. Whenever we talked about faith, he very cleverly kept his distance. He called himself a sceptic and could be very cynical about Christianity. He was raised in a Christian home, but it was a large family and he grew up feeling like he was just a number. He couldn't imagine God having a personal interest in him. He had several relationships, but they failed. His business ran aground. He felt deserted by his friends after spending some time in prison. His drinking problem grew. One evening I visited a pub and he happened to be sitting at the bar. He was groggy from drinking and hopelessly sad, without having words to express it. When he saw me, he was so happy he threw his arm around me and exclaimed, 'I've missed you!'

I recognized the easy friendliness and loose limbs that alcohol can produce. 'How's that? Why did you miss me?'

Luuk replied, 'I don't want to be lost. I've been thinking about it and I need a pastor, a spiritual leader. Gerard, that makes you one lucky b--rd. Sorry to put it that way, but it's the truth. Do you mind me saying that?'

If I had not been used to barroom language, I would have been shocked. It would have paralyzed me; I would've heard the words, but missed their meaning. As we learn to listen to what people really mean, we discover God can give us openings at unexpected moments. I had never heard Luuk say anything like this before. Even when he was drunk, he usually managed to dodge away from my attempts to talk about faith. Could he be serious this time? I promised I'd call him in a few days to make an appointment. I usually do that. Then I can make contact early in the day, when the alcohol has not yet taken over. Also, letting a few days pass between promising to call and actually calling allows people to think twice. If they're really interested, they'll wait for your call and want that appointment. For instance, that same evening, a another drunk fellow called Tom was all over me, too. He wrapped his arm around my neck, breathing into my face in a way that left me gasping for pure oxygen, and babbled, 'Gerard, you're such a great guy. I was thinking last Wednesday, I'm going to Vrooland's Bible study, but you know, my leg isn't doing that well. But... uh... I'll be there next time. Not for the God stuff, mind you - I'm a believer, but the reason I'm coming is that I like you.'

Tom's whole attitude was different from Luuk's. Tom shows up now and again. Like he always used to. But he's not a real seeker. In his case, I may have to wait until he's on his deathbed. Waiting until that very last moment is also part of our calling.

But Luuk was different. Ten days after his cry for help at the bar, we met at Building 33. He was sober and he told me how glad he was that I'd called him. I asked him whether he could remember what he had said to me that night, offering some help by repeating his words: 'I don't want to be lost. I've been thinking about it and I need a pastor, a spiritual leader. Gerard, that makes you...' I looked him straight in the eye and saw him hesitate. What was he to say? After a few moments he found the answer: 'That makes you one lucky guy!'

We had a good laugh together about this unusual introduction. After Luuk had told me some more about himself, stressing that a regular church was no place for him, I shared a few of the options I could offer. He opted for a group whose members he knew from the bar and with whom he knew he would feel quite comfortable. We prayed. Then Luuk did something uncharacteristic. Sitting there on the sofa, he burst into tears.

I was thankful we had a group Luuk could join, but I know it would take a lot more. Luuk needed a fellowship in which he would be able to grow. He was young, with a lifetime of possibilities before him. I realized there were dozens more like Luuk, in search of spiritual nourishment. We also needed a solid safety net for other young folk, like Tom and his wandering friends, too. In other words: it was time to start a COTS fellowship.

In the years that led up to this moment we had been blessed richly. In a sense, the fellowship already existed. By the summer of 2011, we had services in the pub once a month as well as five different Bible study groups. There was a core group of over thirty-six people, including our pastoral team of six. In addition to these, there were another thirty individuals who attended group meetings on a more or less regular basis. And then there was a wider circle of people who felt somehow connected to us: we had their addresses and paid them regular visits. Still others - I would say about a hundred people - dropped in on our pub meetings or group sessions once in a while.

A part of God's great painting

Was this not enough? Why did we need a COTS fellowship that would function as an independent church? Because it is part of gathering in the sheep that belong to Jesus and being part of His worldwide flock - a flock that is as colorful and varied as the endless creativity of the heavenly Artist Himself. We are invited to discover this colorful and 'manifold wisdom' (Eph. 3:10) in all its variegations. All the different shades are a part of that great, worldwide painting of God's saving work through the ages. COTS is just a tiny touch of paint in that great work of art. But whenever a person connects to that small piece, he or she connects to the greater whole! These connections do not just bind people together here on earth, they reach into the spiritual realm, too. We believed they would gain strength if we took an official step towards something that could be recognized by the greater whole as a part of the big picture. That's why institutionalizing COTS mattered. It meant gaining official recognition by the greater whole.

In all of these things, we learn to respond to God's communicative creativity. Developing the right language and customs is decisive in conveying the message. This means we must adapt our church language and customs to the people we are trying to reach. We are not bound to a language, but to the message! If the language and proceedings common to organized churches are a hindrance to our listeners, we must find new ways of communicating with them. But we must never let go of the principles of gathering in the flock. We are bound to the worldwide school of Jesus. The awareness of this can only be conveyed through the use of the universal sacraments: baptism and holy communion. At COTS, we seek to administer these sacraments in a very personal way. In my understanding, celebrating communion should always be accompanied by a personal exhortation to follow Jesus with greater commitment and to give up bad habits. This calls for words that accentuate how Jesus desires to work in us by binding us to one another and to all believers worldwide.

Most of the folks who attend our groups are not readers. It is the vivid imagery of baptism and communion that speaks to their hearts. Visual aids and personal conversations are the ingredients we apply most in these groups. In this context, films based on Bible stories are a great asset. In some of our groups, we usually spend an hour and a half or longer watching part of a film. As we see Abram leave everything behind to journey to an unknown land, and watch him struggle as he leaves the home of his fathers simply because he has heard a voice, we ask those present whether they, too, are ready to let go of things. We ask them whether or not they have heard God's voice in their lives - and whether they know what it is they must leave behind. We talk about what might hinder them from doing this. The visual and the personal work together. From that point of view, baptism and communion are indispensable tools for bringing the message home to people.

We will always be disciples

As our groups grew, our pastoral team began to see more and more clearly how vital an attitude of humility is to our work. We're all disciples; we're all still learning. An awareness of this became a criterion for participation. One Sunday afternoon a lady joined one of our groups. She was lonely in her faith and she was looking for 'a body in which to function,' she told us. She also mentioned that the Lord had taught her many things, which she now wanted to pass on to us. Her contribution fuelled debates, and her impersonal attitude caused irritation. People began to get the feeling she was above the group. We didn't know what to do. But she enjoyed the meetings and wanted to attend our Wednesday group as well. I slept badly that night, praying for wisdom. Did I have the right to bar this lonely believer from our meetings? On what grounds? It didn't seem like a very Christian thing to do. But why did her presence arouse so much resistance? Did the irritation stem from some bad source, or was she the one with the wrong attitude? What would Jesus have done? As I prayed, I began to understand that Jesus' first priority was to make disciples. Those who came to Him as masters rather than as disciples had no need of Him as their Teacher. Those who came to heal others rather than to be cured of their own weaknesses and infirmities had no need of Jesus the Physician.

I contacted the other members of our pastoral team and shared my thoughts with them. Together we decided we wanted to stick to Jesus' Great Commission (Matt. 28:19). We wanted to make disciples and to be disciples. We wanted to receive His strength in our weakness (2 Cor. 12:9), sharing and learning together. One person might have more to give than another, but we were all disciples of Jesus. It became our mission:

1. To make and to be disciples.
2. To baptize and to live as children of the Father, having been cleansed by the Son and under the guidance of the Spirit.
3. To teach one another to 'observe all things I have commanded you' (Matt. 28:19), that is, to demonstrate the practical obedience released in us through the celebration of communion: He in us and we in Him.

First and foremost, we wanted to be, and to make, disciples willing to be led towards baptism and renewal through holy communion with Him.

The official founding of COTS

Sunday, September 18, 2011, was to be the big day. The two pastors who were to ordain the COTS council had told us they could be there by 7 pm. We felt blessed that the new pastor of the Dutch Reformed Church in Sliedrecht had agreed to participate in the inauguration. Two other pastors from churches in the region were also going to be there. The top floor of Building 33 was filled to overflowing with about eighty people. We especially wanted the members of our five groups and those who regularly attended our pub services to be there. But other folks who felt a connection with COTS turned up as well. We presented our communion set and although until that point we had baptized adults by immersion, we were also given a baptismal font. We expect it will be used sooner or later, as we have decided to be open to the various baptism practices prevalent in the different churches. These gifts were given to us by a church that had been closed. We were very pleased with them, as we are eager to be a part of the work of gathering in which Jesus has been doing through the ages.

In one place the doors of a church were closed, while in Sliedrecht a new door was opened. Both were bound together by the same communion cup and the same baptism ceremony. God does not stop. The order of the inauguration service was simple and geared to our colorful community. After we had sung three songs, one of the pastors delivered a short sermon. Then another pastor gave a brief talk on what is expected of elders. After that, the official ordination took place. The pastor from Sliedrecht offered a word of encouragement. I added a thought on stepping out in weakness in order for God's power to be made manifest. Then I said we would sing some more, after which coffee would be served. I had hardly finished the sentence, when a regular bar visitor exclaimed, 'Finally some coffee!'

This was just one of a variety of reactions we had to the service. It was interesting to listen to these reactions over coffee. People accustomed to going to church were very appreciative. Those who never went to church generally felt it could have been a lot shorter - an apt illustration of the fact that at COTS we must find our own ways of dealing with the Word. The individuals who were ordained as elders felt very encouraged. Their joy was mine. But the whole experience also made me feel small, even insecure. The enemy was attacking me. In self-defense, I considered what God had done in the lives of those present, such as the participants in our Sunday services. What did the inauguration mean to them? A lot of the young people who hung out at Building 33 had turned up for the service. I looked around for members of our other groups, noting, to my delight, that they accounted for about half of the total number of people present at the inauguration. I took this to mean they really wanted to be a part of COTS. But did they?

Doubts and misgivings

Doubts and misgivings are never nice. I started listing who was not there. I started weighing every comment. A church person who had not been invited said it was all well and good, but this could never be a real church, because we had ordained women as elders. I picked up a rumor running around the church that pastor Vrooland had finally started running his own show. Yet another person teasingly complained to a team member that I had given too much attention to a friend of his and neglected him. It was meant as a joke, but it still made me think. Carolien's mind was full of memories of the difficulties that had led us to this step. My son and daughter had mixed feelings, too. The organized church had caused them pain and sorrow in the preceding years - and now their parents were setting up a new one? Tears flowed. I felt myself being tossed back and forth. Sure,

I could understand all those people. I knew about the painful memories. But I wanted to rejoice in what God had given us. At the same time, I felt guilty for refusing to shed a tear over the past. Wasn't it a miracle that any of this had happened? Who could have expected it? We had been through so many troubles with the Dutch Reformed Church of Sliedrecht, yet today we had received a wonderful blessing from representatives of its council! The regional churches shared in our excitement! So many members of our groups had turned up! Of course, I missed certain people and, of course, there was nothing wrong with reliving pain of past events - but I did not want to focus on any of that. I wanted to enthrone the Lord, my God, who inhabits our praises (Ps. 22:3).

Our words can go two different ways. We can use them to build a throne for the One or for the other. I believe grumbling and complaining raises a throne for God's enemy. Of course, some tears are a part of our search for God (Luke 7:38; Heb. 5:7). But Scripture focuses more on how to overcome sorrow by finding our joy in His strength (Phil. 4:4-7). By doing this we enter into the realm of God's peace, or, in other words, into the sphere of His throne. The more attention we pay to Satan's successes, the more power his throne acquires in our lives.

The road we travelled was not always easy. Mulling over past afflictions could easily have gotten me into a vicious circle of negativity. I could have started feeling down about the fact that some folks had not taken the trouble to be there on September 18, even though they had promised they would. But if I gave in to those feelings, I would be focusing on the devil's victories. In my grumbling, I would be building a throne for the one whose goal is to destroy the work of God. He would appear stronger than our Savior. The devil likes to impose his successes on us, but I don't want to honor him. He doesn't deserve it.

We will no doubt face more troubles and resistance in the future, but if I observe the works of the devil it will only be from the corner of my eye. I won't ignore them, but I want to view them with the absolute certainty that they are his last convulsions.

> 'I will declare thy name unto my brethren:
> in the midst of the congregation will I praise thee.
> Ye that fear the LORD, praise him!'
>
> (Ps. 22:22-23)

God has brought us this far

So we founded COTS. Where things will go from here, we don't know. The groups are growing. We just added a new one. I couldn't persuade its members to come to Building 33, so instead, every two weeks, I visit their hangout in an apartment. The group has about eight members now. Two of them want to be baptized. There will be more developments like this, I'm sure. And more problems, too. How we will solve those, we don't know. As for money, we don't know where that will come from either. We have no idea who will join us. What we do know is that God has brought us this far. We embrace uncertainties as 'infirmities' to glory in (2 Cor. 12:9). Glorying in infirmities is something we have to learn. One source of inspiration is the wisdom of C.A. Schwarz (*Natural Church Development*). He highlights working with small groups. It is an effective way of equipping and challenging people to discover their gifts - and put them to work.

We have a core of highly committed people. I like to see them as the center of COTS, with wider circles spreading out from there. The people in the outer circles are less committed: the further out, the less the involvement. The outermost circle consists of people we can only reach through prayer and care. We have a large group of prayer supporters. They carry these people in their prayers. We don't have a membership roll. We don't want COTS to become a regular organized church. We do see what God is doing in people's lives. As their commitment grows, they will start proving themselves to be true members of the Body. You don't need to be a church member to be a member of Christ's Body. The Spirit shapes the Body and we receive whatever the Spirit gives. We use certain rituals, such as anointing, to confirm people in a specific position. But our movements are always in direct response to visible growth, or a longing for growth. This is how we have appointed elders and deacons so far: in response to the love and commitment they have demonstrated, we have given them the honor of those positions. We have been blessed beyond imagination thus far. But we know full well we must not get blinded by the blessings we've received.

When Jesus' disciples returned from their first outreach, they were wild with enthusiasm. Amazing things had happened. They had been blessed beyond their wildest dreams. They had healed the sick and performed miracles. Even evil spirits had fled in the name of Jesus. But Jesus led them away from their preoccupation with all the mighty deeds they had done in His name. He said: '(…) in this rejoice not, that the spirits are subject unto you; but rather rejoice because your names are written in heaven' (Luke 10:17-20). That is our joy!

'Lord, thank You! You look upon us in grace and love! Will You use us? May our service cause many more names to be written in the book of life You have stored up in heaven.'

Appendix 1. The Good Samaritan

A sermon on Luke 10 & HC[16] Sunday 12

On May 10, 2011, Carolien and I decided I would no longer travel around the country every Sunday to preach. There were two reasons. On the one hand, our work at COTS was gaining momentum. On the other hand, I was having more and more difficulty with preaching. Almost every Sunday I would arrive back home feeling my message had not come across at all. I missed having conversations in which I could find out what people had picked up.

I kept asking myself whether preaching had any effect at all and if it did, how that effect could be monitored. Surely, we should be able to see the Word at work! Maybe the Spirit was using my sermons, but I couldn't tell. Perhaps I wanted too much? I'm sure that's true to some extent - but if preachers stop wanting to see their sermons have an effect on people, churches should start getting worried! I was blessed myself by my sermon preparation, but that wasn't my goal. In my last month of preaching, the sermon I will share with you in this Appendix is the only one I delivered. It is one I want to have firmly anchored in my own heart. As it echoes the contents of this book, I have included it here. It would be wonderful if you and other readers would start following the example of the Good Samaritan - then this sermon, at least, will have made an impact. The sermon is about what we as Christians can learn from the Samaritan man. First, let's read the story as it is told in Luke 10; then we will read Sunday 12 and I'll share my sermon.

Luke 10 - The parable of the Good Samaritan

Luke 10:25-37: 'And, behold, a certain lawyer stood up, and tempted him, saying, Master, what shall I do to inherit eternal

---
[16] Heidelberg Catechism.

life? He said unto him, What is written in the law? how readest thou? And he answering said, Thou shalt love the Lord thy God with all thy heart, and with all thy soul, and with all thy strength, and with all thy mind; and thy neighbour as thyself. And he said unto him, Thou hast answered right: this do, and thou shalt live. But he, willing to justify himself, said unto Jesus, And who is my neighbour? And Jesus answering said, A certain *man* went down from Jerusalem to Jericho, and fell among thieves, which stripped him of his raiment, and wounded *him*, and departed, leaving *him* half dead. And by chance there came down a certain priest that way: and when he saw him, he passed by on the other side. And likewise a Levite, when he was at the place, came and looked *on him*, and passed by on the other side. But a certain Samaritan, as he journeyed, came where he was: and when he saw him, he had compassion *on him*, And went to *him*, and bound up his wounds, pouring in oil and wine, and set him on his own beast, and brought him to an inn, and took care of him. And on the morrow when he departed, he took out two pence, and gave *them* to the host, and said unto him, Take care of him; and whatsoever thou spendest more, when I come again, I will repay thee. Which now of these three, thinkest thou, was neighbour unto him that fell among the thieves? And he said, He that shewed mercy on him. Then said Jesus unto him, Go, and do thou likewise.'

Heidelberg Catechism Sunday 12
Question & answer 32

Question: Why are you called a Christian?

Answer: Because I am a member of Christ by faith and thus share in His anointing, so that I may as prophet confess His name, as priest present myself a living sacrifice of thankfulness to Him, and as king fight with a free and good conscience against sin and the devil in this life, and hereafter reign with Him eternally over all creatures.

Dear friends,

Is this not a strange combination? On the one hand, the Catechism; on the other, this Samaritan. In many churches, the Catechism is a symbol of orthodoxy. Orthodoxy is important to us. But we know the Samaritans added elements to their faith that were absolutely unorthodox! In those days, the temple was the center of Jewish faith. But the Samaritans held a different view. An unorthodox view. The Jews had the true temple in those days, not the Samaritans. The Samaritan confession was all wrong on this important issue! Yet Jesus chose to use a Samaritan in His parable! It is as if Jesus deliberately wanted to pierce through all outward appearances:

'Not he who hears My words and correctly repeats them is wise, but who obeys My words... he is the one who lives out the true confession!'

Jesus often used examples like this one. Once He used the queen of Sheba as an example. She visited Solomon to listen to his wisdom - unlike the Jews, who were unwilling to listen to Jesus. He also mentioned the people of Nineveh. They repented the moment Jonah began to preach! The Jews in Jesus' day didn't. He spoke of Naaman, the widow of Zarephath, the Gentile centurion, the Canaanite woman - all Gentile examples for us to follow. Jesus is not fooled by outward appearances. By using these examples, He shows us He is not interested in fine words, but in sincerity of heart. This is how He came to use the example of the Samaritan in this parable.

Before we take a closer look at the parable, I'd like to consider answer 32.

The question is: What characterizes a Christian?
The answer: He partakes in the Spirit of Christ.

In the text, the word anointing is used, but it is a reference to the work of the Spirit.

Through this Spirit we confess His name; wholly sacrifice ourselves to Him; fight against sin and the devil with a free and good conscience, and receive eternal life.

This last point is no mere trifle. Eternal life… now that is something! To live forever in the eternal glory or… to suffer eternal condemnation and death. The question, then, is:

What are you, a genuine Christian or a fake Christian? The answer has eternal consequences.

In Luke we read that a lawyer came to Jesus with this question: 'What shall I do to inherit eternal life?' What led this man to ask this question? The things he had heard. He knew the disciples were healing the sick and casting out demons in the name of Jesus. They were doing it all over the place. Healing and deliverance in Jesus' name. And this lawyer then heard Jesus say His disciples should rejoice in the fact that their names were written in the book of eternal life. That was the most important thing, He said. This Jesus was acting as if He knew things only God could know! It was that combination of enabling people to do amazing things in His name and saying His disciples should rejoice in the eternal life they had received. As if Jesus knew!

This lawyer didn't trust Jesus. He wasn't sure about His teaching. So he asked Jesus: 'What shall I do to inherit eternal life?' Note that this man was a lawyer. He was probably thinking: 'Nowhere does the law suggest that we must cast out demons to receive eternal life! So this Jesus can't be right! What strange powers are at work in Him? He offers healing to even the worst of sinners: prostitutes and tax collectors! He goes around freely offering grace and forgiveness as if there is no law! How does this Jesus interpret the law, I wonder? What would He say I must do to inherit eternal life?' That was the lawyer's question.

Jesus replied: 'Alright, do you want to know? What does the law state? What does it say?'

The man answered immediately: 'Thou shalt love the Lord thy God with all thy heart, and with all thy soul, and with all thy strength, and with all thy mind; and thy neighbour as thyself.'

'Good! Go and do that and you will live!'

The lawyer was somewhat taken aback. Was it that simple? Jesus made no mention at all of miracles and wonders. Only of love. That was the heart of the matter. All we must do, He said, was simply to share love.

The lawyer, wanting to prove things couldn't be that easy, asked another question: who is my neighbor? He wanted to find out whom to love and whom not to love.

'Wait a minute,' Jesus said. 'I'll explain it with a story. A man went down to Jericho. On the way, he was attacked by thieves. They grabbed him, beat him up, tore his clothes from his body and left him lying there, more dead than alive. This poor man needed help, or he would die. Luckily, a priest happened to come by! The priest saw the man... and got a fright. He walked on, giving the victim a wide berth! Then a Levite appeared. He, too, saw the man. And he, too, passed by!'

What was going on here?

Let's go back to the Catechism. It says Christians are to confess the name of Jesus as prophets. Christians - the very name refers to Christ. We bear the name of Christ. We often forget this. It has huge implications. Imagine you were to act the way the priest and the Levite did. You bear the name of

Christ. People who see you, see the name of Jesus, it is written all over you, as it were. You are a Christian, a representative of Him. This means people will look for Christ in you, and rightly so. Imagine you were to avoid people in need of help, just like the priest and the Levite did. Some Christians want to preach to people in need. They preach, while ignoring their needs. And they call that confessing the name of Jesus. It's more like ridiculing and dishonoring the name of Jesus!

Just imagine... From the corner of his eye, the wounded man sees a priest go by, then a Levite. These men were committed to the name of God. They were representatives of God, yet they walked by. What do you think this man would have felt about God at that moment? That God didn't care one bit about his situation! That God probably had far more important matters on His mind. Yes, perhaps that was it: the priest was on his way to Jerusalem to sacrifice! But he wasn't. He was on his way 'down.' That means he was heading for Jericho.

But wait a minute. A priest was not supposed to touch a dead person. The wounded man lying by the roadside looked more dead than alive. What if the priest offered to help him and the latter suddenly died in his arms? That would make the priest unclean, unfit for the service of God. Was that why he didn't help the man? Think about it. What message, what confession, would that convey? That God is far more interested in temple rituals than in the world's suffering! Is that what God is like? Is that what the temple is for? Is that true celebration? Do you think going to church services is more important than helping people on the street? Did Jesus not leave the most beautiful worship service behind when He left heaven to help us?

Perhaps it was natural to think the wounded man had only just been attacked and that the thieves were still around. Danger! Keep away! If that is our attitude as God's representatives, we are suggesting God is not willing to take any risks in order to save us. Is that what God is like? Does God flee from life-threatening situations?

The same could be said for the Levite. Perhaps he was on his way to the temple. He had responsibilities there, along with the other Levites. I'm sure they could have done the job without him for once. But to him, serving in the temple was more important than helping a man on the brink of death. It may seem very pious. We might think this Levite loved God so much, he just didn't have time to think about those in need. Big mistake! Just read what the Old Testament prophets have to say about that (Is. 1:13-17 Amos 5:21-27 et cetera). They repeatedly point out how God loathes people who come to worship Him while neglecting those in need. God said: 'First love your neighbor, then worship Me. Only then can I have fellowship with you. Only then will you demonstrate that you understand the real meaning of worship.'

We were not put on this earth to talk about God's Kingdom; we were put here to demonstrate its power! That's why Jesus sent His disciples out to heal the sick. They shared His healing power liberally and said, 'The kingdom of God has come to you. Look, healing for you, deliverance for you!' (Is. 58:6-10) Of course, we are to love God above all else and with all we have. But we must do it by sharing God's lovingkindness with those around us! By seeing the suffering on the streets. And not just by seeing, but by being a neighbor to those in need.

Do you know the meaning of the word neighbor? It is derived from the word near, or nigh. God wants us to care so much about other people that we long to draw near to them. The best way to honor God is to treat others as precious loved ones, as people who are near to us, like our children or partner.

This is how our Savior came to this earth. He came in search of those near to Him. He came for His bride! He went around blessing people and noting their response. That's how

He discovered His bride, for whom He was willing to sacrifice everything.

Who are you willing to give your life for? Who are you willing to suffer loneliness and the pains of hell for? Only for those who are nearest to you. That's what Jesus did.

The priest and the Levite undoubtedly confessed the name of God with their lips. But their actions told a different story: they neglected one of His precious children. I believe this is why churches are on the decline. Church people, traditionally, often tend to focus on having the right confession and the right religion. We also have a tendency to wallow in our sinfulness and fret about our salvation. This has often kept us from breaking out of the circle of our own existence. It has often dictated our worship services. We should have been busy loving our neighbors instead! Of course, we have to keep fighting against sin and the devil. But have you ever asked yourself what would be the most effective way of doing that? The best approach is to set aside our selfishness and break out of our own little world. How do we let in the devil's influence? By closing our eyes to the needs of those around us. That's what the devil does: he ignores human suffering. Let them suffer, he says!

What do we do when we see someone in need? How do we respond? Are we the first to help, like Jesus was? Or do we prefer to wait and see: 'Wow... that looks scary. Better not go near. Besides, I have so much important stuff to do. And I probably can't do anything anyway. Never mind...'

Whenever that is our response, we are giving in to the sin of fear. The Bible tells us, in Revelation, that 'the fearful' will not enter the heavenly Jerusalem. We all have our moments of fear. But giving in is cowardly and can cost us our position in the heavenly Jerusalem (Rev. 21:8). The battle against sin and the devil is very real. Overcome your fear. Face the needs around you and give whatever it takes.

Look at what the Samaritan did. That's what Jesus wants to see in us. He wants us to hold up His name. That's what

Christians do! Christians aren't afraid of robbers that might be lurking nearby. They're not stopped by differences. Remember, the victim was a Jew, and Jews and Samaritans in those days hated each other! Don't let cultural or emotional barriers stop you.

The Samaritan man was on a journey, perhaps a business trip. 'Well, don't worry about money and profit margins - there's someone in need over there!' He saw the victim lying there. He went over. He noticed he was still alive. It touched him... He got some oil and wine to treat the man's wounds and prevent infections. The wounds were so numerous, he used all his oil and wine. 'No worries, this guy needs it!' He treated the man as a close relative. He bound up his wounds. He let the Jew ride his mount, while he walked the rest of the way. He led him to a kind of hotel, taking time to care for him properly. He didn't rest until he felt confident the Jew was going to make it.

The next day he went to the hotel manager and paid him for two days of full service. He wanted to make sure his friend received the best treatment. 'Take care of him; and whatsoever thou spendest more, when I come again, I will repay thee.'

Then that other question popped up. Instead of offering the lawyer a precise answer to his question, 'And who is my neighbor?,' Jesus responded with a deeper question: 'To whom will you draw near? Which openings do you see for being a neighbor?'

Jesus' actual question was: 'Which now of these three, thinkest thou, was neighbour unto him that fell among the thieves?' In other words, 'Which of the passers-by seized the opportunity to draw near?'

The lawyer answered, 'He that shewed mercy on him.' Then said Jesus, 'Go, and do thou likewise.'

Stop and think about this for a moment. What an unusual question! This is what Jesus was asking the lawyer: 'Who was allowed to get nearest to the victim?' Three men had seen the victim. The first was a man of God. As a priest, he bore God's name. As a neighbor, he should have come right alongside the victim. But instead, the victim looked up into the priest's eyes and saw horror.

The second man was also a servant of God. He, too, should have drawn near to the wounded Jew. But his face expressed abhorrence as well. It was like some devilish grimace.

Both of these men were official bearers of God's name. How terrible. Yet this is reality. And if this happens in the church, it's no wonder the church falls into decline. The spiritual damage is huge: devilish features on the faces of God's servants.

The third man, the Samaritan, lived worlds apart from the Jew. They were enemies! It's not unlikely that the victim was afraid to look up when he saw the Samaritan - afraid of getting another beating maybe. But when he looked into the eyes of the Samaritan, what did he see? He saw the eyes of Christ! He saw a burning love, a deep compassion, a willingness to take any risk, just to save the man's life.

That's how much Jesus cares about us. His desire to see us happy is far greater. He wants to be nearer to us than anyone. I love to think of His kind eyes looking upon us so lovingly. It's beautiful.

Our eyes and attitudes should reflect the heart of Jesus. That's what it means to confess His name, to give ourselves to Him. It is our privilege, our duty, to share His love liberally wherever we go. That's what Jesus told the lawyer to do. The lawyer had heard that Jesus' disciples were going around casting out evil spirits and healing the sick. Perhaps now he would come to understand what it meant to freely share God's grace. Sadly, he did not. But we can. We can understand this beautiful, life-changing generosity.

Jesus told the disciples to rejoice in the fact that their names were written in the book of life. But how did their names get to be written there? The reason was that Jesus had come near to them, had become their nearest one, in order to give them eternal life. He is the incarnation of the temple service. Everything that happened in the temple can be found in Him, and is available for us to give out freely on the street: forgiveness, grace, the power of love and salvation. That is what Jesus wants to do through us. Like a true neighbor, Jesus offers us all the goodness of God. 'Thank You, Lord! We need Your care, Your work in us. You want to carry us home on Your donkey, as it were, and to help us fully recover from life's beatings and bruises. And You want to bear the punishment for the beatings we've given others, too.'

The lawyer, meanwhile, had probably gone back to brooding on the doctrinal correctness of all this. We spend a lot of brooding on things, too. Our sins, church affairs, family issues, all the things that go wrong in our lives. We talk about the attacks and temptations of the devil. But we need to stop doing that. We have a neighbor, One near to us, who cares for us. Go in His strength and demonstrate the power of His name. That's how to fight sin and the devil. He will pick us up and carry us home. Our names are in the book of life!

The Catechism says we can fight the battle with a free and good conscience. Let's do that, the way we're told to in Luke 10. Show the face of Jesus in our walking and talking. What a wonderful challenge. That's how we can show we're Christians. 'Lord, teach us through Your Spirit!' Amen.

Appendix 2. Thirteen conversation pointers

In this appendix, you will find the conversation pointers we discuss in our discipleship school classes on street work.

1. A cry for help is the overture to a conversion call.

I've learned that in personal conversations it is best to be cautious about giving a conversion call. In the Bible, the call to conversion follows an urgent cry for help: 'What shall we do?' (Acts 2:37) If you rush the call, accidents will happen. For one thing, you will unintentionally place yourself above the other person.

The moment you take the position of someone already converted, suggesting in word or attitude that the other person needs converting, too, you will create distance and spark resistance. An attitude like that reveals a lack of humility. But even if, in all humility, you feel you must urge the other person towards conversion, you may be casting pearls before swine - which will irritate those swine and cause them to turn on you! Telling a person he or she is 'not yet ready for conversion' is another recipe for irritation; it may well ruin your chances of making any real progress in the relationship.

2. Look for the prodigal son position.

People will only change position if, like the prodigal son, they become convinced that their current position is not viable and the new position looks much better. In the case of the prodigal son, this meant returning to his father. This means we must look for a person's real need. Then that person can bear his soul and we can offer an invitation to conversion. It is also important to show through your lifestyle that a new life with God is better than the old life.

3. Be aware of the difference between judge and father.

Charges and condemnation belong to the language of a judge. In conversations, we are often tempted to take the position of a jury and pass judgment on all sorts of abuses. There is a place for words of this nature, in relation to both ourselves and others. We're all sinners. But a conversation can get stuck on condemnation and punishment. Words of forgiveness and a loving embrace, by contrast, belong to the language of a father. They create openings in conversations.

God is both Judge and Father. We may allow room for guilt when unbelievers or others condemn themselves. Denial is unscriptural (1 John 1:8-10). But be sensitive to the nature of the condemnation. If people have been deeply hurt, the road to forgiveness can be tough. A person who speaks bitterly about others may not be open to the forgiving attitude of the Father. Speaking about God in that way to such a person is like throwing pearls before swine. If a person is deeply concerned about his own guilt, a pastoral journey towards the Father can begin.

When guilt issues emerge, don't clamp onto the forgiveness of the Father too quickly. But as soon as you can, you will be in a good position in the conversation. The other person will get to know the Father through you. This will enable him to start seeking Him personally as well as introducing Him to others.

When faced with condemnation, try to get personal: 'I can imagine you feel this way. If you were a judge, your reaction would be the right one. Evildoers must be punished. Every judge would agree on that. But what if the guilty one were your child? Would you reject your child like that? Or would you do everything within your power to help? That's what a father does!'

4. Look to receive a blessing from God through the other person and remember your relationship with him or her is reciprocal.

This pointer will keep you from thinking everything depends on you. For starters, everything you have to offer comes from the Sender (Matt. 10:1). Be vulnerable in approaching the other person, just as your Sender sends you. Your vulnerability will give the other person something to respond to caringly (Matt. 10:9-10). We need to learn to receive God's blessings through other people. Try to discover whether the other person is open to having fellowship with you in celebration of the good things of God (Matt. 10:11-14). Then the principle of the Body of Christ will be at work from the very beginning. You will be giving to others, and they will be giving right back to you. We all need each other. If there is no reciprocity, you will almost always get off on a wrong footing.

5. Connect with the preparatory work the Spirit has already done.

Ask yourself whether you recognize any traces of God's love in the person you are talking to, or in his family, friends or pets. Show him these qualities come from God and that God, being the source of all good things, embodies them to the very highest degree and shares them freely with people. Acknowledge that the good things people do, have their origins in God. Praise what is good and express your enjoyment of the fact that it reflects God's work.

6. Discussions easily spark bigotry.

'What is your purpose in life?' 'What is the meaning of it all?' 'What will happen to you when you die?' 'Do you believe in anything?' 'Do you think there is a God who will bring justice? Could there even be justice if there were no God to pass final judgment?'

These are all good ways of starting a conversation about faith. However, they all carry the risk of placing you and your conversation partner at opposite ends of the table. Especially if you start trying to track down the errors in his or her reasoning. If your aim is to prove that your views are superior, you will invite the other person to take on the same attitude. Before you know it, bigotry will drive you apart. By pointing out what you like about the other person's ideas, on the other hand, and suggesting it reflects the goodness of God, you will build bridges. You will soon have a secure position from which to cultivate the relationship. You can also respond to desires for good and beautiful things, while pointing out the destructive - or even diabolical - power of evil things. A longing for things not within reach can lead the conversation towards the human need for salvation. Then you can explain your belief that only Jesus can fulfil that need.

7. Encourage people to find their own answers by asking the right questions.

The fewer the answers you give, the less likely you are to place yourself above another person. The more answers the other person offers, the more he will be likely to own them. Then you can express agreement on his statements, saying they appeal to you because they are like the things God says. You could even suggest that God is speaking right into the other person's heart through these thoughts and answers.

8. Look for the intentions behind sharp questions.

If a person starts coming at you with sharp questions - such as, 'If God is a God of love, then why...' - ask him whether his purpose is to find real answers or to keep God at a distance. When the Samaritan woman started quizzing Jesus on a theological issue, her real intention was to hide her history of broken relationships (John 4). People often use theological questions to shield themselves from life's real questions.

9. Watch for good and bad seed.

People's lives are like fields in which good and bad seed is sown (Matt. 13:24-26, Gal. 6:7-9). You can't force the growth of good seed in another person's life any more than you can uproot bad seed. What you can do is encourage him to recognize the difference himself, so that he can nourish the good and eliminate the bad. For instance, if a person is angry at the church, try and find out the root cause. It may well be something God is angry about, too. If it is, acknowledge the justness of this anger, while also encouraging him not to allow anger to prevent him from seeing the good of the church and hindering his own growth. If you see love in a person, that's great. But be careful to discern whether it is love or something else, like an addiction. People can mislead themselves with false passions. Someone who says, 'I am so passionate about our church,' may be quite unprepared to surrender to the will of God or to give himself to building God's Kingdom. Look out for pride, too. If someone is pleased with himself for doing a lot of good work, bless what is good and seek for ways in which you can help him recognize what is not good. Asking good questions will often bring people to a new understanding of things. Use questions to search for a prodigal-son attitude.

10. Don't be afraid of losing a debate, but do be afraid of losing love.

You can admit someone else knows more about a certain topic than you do, or has better arguments, while still holding onto your trust in the power of God's love. Love transcends arguments! Use a personal testimony to share how much He means to you. Add that His love enables you to love others, too. Including the person you're talking to. Then you go on to point out all the beautiful things you appreciate in him. If you do this, you will give him something against which there is no defense. And it will be easier to pick up the conversation next time.

11. Keep holding out your hand faithfully and patiently.

If a conversation does not seem to have led anywhere, but you have a good connection with the other person, be like the father of the prodigal son: he stood on the lookout. You may have to watch and wait for five or ten years before anything happens. Sometimes a contact doesn't yield any growth in the person in question, but other contacts result with people who are more open to the Gospel.

12. Bear in mind that creation reflects God.

Just as the earthly tabernacle, or temple, modeled spiritual truths (Ex. 25:9; 25:40; 27:8), creation also reflects the higher reality of God's deeds and the battle in the heavenly realm (Rom. 1:20; Eph. 6:11-12). Use this parallel in conversations with people who are receptive to them.

13. Take into account that some people will be apprehensive.

If you want to get back to someone at a later point in time, make sure you have his or her phone number. It's easier for you to call a person than for him or her to call you. Most people are apprehensive about extending contact by phone. An invitation to a meeting or some other activity can be even scarier for some. If you do this, get him or her to bring along some friends. Another approach might be for you to pick him or her up so that you can go to the event together. Remember, it is usually easier for people if you look them up in their own surroundings than to be invited to some unknown place and event.

THE END

www.ingramcontent.com/pod-product-compliance
Lightning Source LLC
LaVergne TN
LVHW010203070526
838199LV00062B/4483